PELICAN BOOKS

A241

THE ENGLISH VILLAGE

VICTOR BONHAM-CARTER

D0942979

VICTOR BONHAM-CARTER

The English
Village

WITH A FOREWORD BY DR C. S. ORWIN
AND LINE DRAWINGS
BY HELLMUTH WEISSENBORN

PENGUIN BOOKS

HARMONDSWORTH · MIDDLESEX

FIRST PUBLISHED 1952

To
A. E. B - C.

MADE AND PRINTED IN GREAT BRITAIN
FOR PENGUIN BOOKS LTD
BY WILLIAM CLOWES AND SONS LTD,
LONDON AND BECCLES
COLLOGRAVURE PLATES PRINTED BY
HARRISON AND SONS LTD, LONDON

CONTENTS

LIST OF PLATES

(Between pages 128 and 129)

PREFACE

THIS *might conceivably be described as a guide book, but not in the ordinary sense of the term. It makes no attempt, for instance, to lead you on tour through the counties, nor does it take you to the acknowledged beauty spots. It is not even a reference book, to which you can turn for encyclopaedic information about farming, handicrafts, or the multifarious activities of country life. To fulfil any of these functions adequately would require a very large book, and that is not my aim.*

My purpose is to present the main facts of rural history, and to isolate the constituent elements of English village life. By this means I hope to create a clear unbiased impression of the village, both as a place and as a community; likewise to estimate the part it has to play in the history of the nation. In so far as the countryside has little value without the human activity that goes on there, the village must always remain the focus of all rural life and work. In my view, then, the village is the key to nearly every country problem, and that is why I have made it the subject of this book.

Finally, I am aware that the method of presentation is an arbitrary one, and that there are many omissions, and that this will call for criticism. My action is quite deliberate. I feel strongly the time has come to cut a path through the jungle of rural literature — a literature that grows daily and feeds so much upon the ignorance of the townsman, and upon the affection felt by nearly everyone for the English countryside, whether he lives there or not. In either case, it is so often the countryside that suffers, for neither ignorance nor affection are in themselves appropriate. What is needed first of all is information — then common sense.

VICTOR BONHAM-CARTER

Langaller Farm
   Brushford, Somerset
    June 1951

ACKNOWLEDGEMENTS

IT would be foolish for anybody to attempt a book of this kind without obtaining all the help possible. For this reason I was fortunate in having the assistance of a number of experts to whose ability and generosity I now wish to pay full tribute.

First, the late the Rt Hon. Sir Leslie Scott, who was engaged upon writing a Foreword to the book shortly before his untimely death in May 1950.

Second, Dr C. S. Orwin, who read through the entire MS., offered sound and sage advice, and gave me much encouragement. I wish to thank him sincerely for this, and for the Foreword he has written. Also to say that many of my ideas about village civilization owe something (if not everything) to a long acquaintance with his work.

Third, Mr A. K. Hudson of Bristol University, who gave me a tremendous amount of help in the detailed writing of the book. I drew deeply upon his profound knowledge of the social history of the countryside, and I profited by his recommendations on a hundred points of fact and style. I am indeed grateful.

Next I wish to thank all those who helped me with specific portions of the book:

Part One: Mr and Mrs A. R. Maxwell-Hyslop, and Sir Ben Bowen Thomas, for general historical advice. Mrs Jacquetta Hawkes, and Mr W. A. Seaby, Keeper of Taunton Museum, without whose active help I could never have written Chapter 1 and part of Chapter 2. The executors of the late Sir H. Rider Haggard for permission to make an extended reference in Chapter 7 to the conclusions expressed in *Rural England* (Longmans).

Part Two: Chapter 1: Mr A. D. Hallam, Assistant Keeper of Taunton Museum, for geological information. – Chapter 2: Mr Cosmo Clark and Mr James White, Director and Information Officer, respectively, of the Rural Industries Bureau; and Miss K. S. Woods. – Chapter 3: Mr Eric Major, Secretary of the Parish Councils Association; Mr I. P. Collis, Somerset County Archivist, and his assistant Mr D. L. Mirams; also Mr Harold

Jowitt of Somerset County Council, and Mr H. A. Jewell, Surveyor and Sanitary Inspector of Dulverton Rural District Council. – Chapter 4: Prebendary G. W. Saunders, Vicar of Martock, and the Rev. G. E. Tucker, Rector of Brushford, Somerset, for advice on Church history and architecture. The Rev. Clifford Bozeat, Minister of Marlborough Congregational Church, and the Rev. F. F. Clutterbuck, Methodist Superintendent Minister of the Kingswood Bourne Circuit, Bristol, for advice on the Chapel. Mr J. V. E. Rundle, Headmaster of Bampton Secondary Modern School, Devon, Mr Robert Birley, Headmaster of Eton College, and Dr Arnold Platts, for advice on the School.

Part Three: Mr Thomas Houghton, County Planning Officer of Berkshire, for his comments upon village planning. Mr Richard Heathcoat Amory for helpful conversations regarding the relationship of English agriculture to external trade.

In addition, I wish to thank all those authors and publishers for permission to quote from or otherwise make use of their books. Of these the majority are separately acknowledged in the text, but I desire also to record my thanks to the following:

Dr J. A. Venn, President of Queens' College, Cambridge, for permission to quote a case of Tithe extravagance from his book *Foundations of Agricultural Economics* (C.U.P.). Professor G. M. Trevelyan, Master of Trinity College, Cambridge, for two quotations from his book *English Social History* (Longmans). Dr C. S. Orwin for certain extracts from *Country Planning,* of which he was editor (O.U.P.). Mrs Kathleen Innes for the description of the Flower Show at St Mary Bourne, Hampshire, in her book *Life in a Hampshire Village* (privately printed). Dr Thomas Sharp for help in obtaining illustrations; his two books *The Anatomy of the English Village* (Penguin) and *English Panorama* (Architectural Press) provided much information on the physical development of the village, described in *Part Two,* Chapter 1. Likewise, Mr Marshall Sisson, whose book *Country Cottages* (Methuen) explores much of the same field with a precision that I also have attempted to emulate. Mr W. E. Tate, whose invaluable book *The Parish Chest* (C.U.P.) provided the background for *Part Two,* Chapter 3, and much of Chapter 4. The

Director and Chief Editor of the Bureau of Current Affairs for permission to make use of material appearing in BCA Pamphlets Nos 27 and 69, both written by myself. The Editor of the *Farmers' Weekly* for permission to make use of material appearing in articles written by myself, and for help in obtaining illustrations.

Finally, I wish to extend my grateful thanks to Mr J. E. V. Birch, Borough Librarian, Taunton, for obtaining and allowing me the use of so many books over such a long period of time.

I also wish to express my thanks to all those who have provided me with the illustrations for this book:

Plates: Picture Post Library 1 (a), 2 (b), 7 (b), 8 (a), 8 (b), 11 (a), 11 (b), 14 (a), 14 (b); Ashmolean Museum, Oxford 1 (b); Navana Studios, Taunton 3; Aerofilms Ltd 4, 5; Swindon Press 6 (a); Topical Press Agency 6 (b); Mr Douglas Went, Brightlingsea 7 (a); Mr H. Smith, Westcliff-on-Sea 9; Gainsborough Studios, Tiverton 10 (a), 10 (b); Central Office of Information (Crown copyright) 13; Mr John Pearce, Cornwall Council of Social Service 15 (a); Rural Industries Bureau 16 (a), 16 (b); Mr P. Swainsbury, Brushford 12 (a–d); Mr F. C. Strutt, Newbury 2 (a), 15 (b).

Line Drawings: Dr Thomas Sharp for the plans of the villages of Coxwold and Heighington, reproduced from his book *The Anatomy of the Village* (Penguin Books); Professor Stuart Piggott and Messrs Chatto & Windus for the Plan and Isometric Reconstruction of the Neolithic House at Haldon, Devon, reproduced from *Prehistoric Britain,* by Christopher and Jacquetta Hawkes; the Editor of *Antiquity,* and Mr and Mrs Hawkes, for the Roman Farm at Lockleys, Welwyn. Reconstruction after excavation, etc.; Mr Sydney Jones for certain technical advice; Dr Hellmuth Weissenborn for the excellence of his work as principal illustrator.   V. B.-C.

FOREWORD

by C. S. Orwin

How many people, I wonder, have given more than a passing thought to the effects of the economic and social revolution of the twentieth century on the English countryside? Its results in the industrial centres have been obvious to everyone, and all too late the State has taken powers to control and direct their further development. In the smaller country towns, the villages, and hamlets the changes have been equally revolutionary, though passing with little general notice because they have been manifest, until very recently, in the decline rather than in the growth of social life, and in the contraction rather than in the expansion of economic opportunity.

People still living can remember the days when the English villages, most of them, were almost entirely self-contained, supplying all the wants of their people according to the standards of the times. They were the days before home agriculture had declined, had indeed temporarily collapsed, calling for reconstruction at a level which drove many farm workers to seek new opportunities in industrial work or in emigration; before public education, the national health services, and the housing schemes of local authorities had displaced voluntary organization and supply by the churches, landowners, and private charity; before the regulation of wages and conditions of work had given the country worker more leisure and more money to spend in its enjoyment; before the mass production of requisites for farm and home, and the universal organization of transport and distribution, had put so many of the rural craftsmen and women out of business; before the supersession of the carrier's cart by the motor bus had opened up a new prospect to every villager on marketing or pleasure bent. They were the days in which each village community was a microcosm, days in which everyone looked to his village to supply him with the means of life, even though it might be at a low level, and opportunities to enjoy it, even though they were few and simple.

The change, in living memory, has been immense. In villages unaffected by urban expansion or by the location of new industries, populations have been halved. Economic opportunity has contracted by the disappearance of most rural industries, while the demand of agriculture for labour has declined heavily, owing to the turnover of the industry, first, from a ploughland to a grassland basis, and, more recently, from a manual to a mechanical art. Social changes, at the same time, have virtually destroyed the openings for young women in domestic work, and for young men in estate work, and in gardens, stables, and so on, once offered by the country houses and the life they stood for. All these depressing effects in the economic life of the villages have had their counterpart in the social life; as the numbers of the community declined, so the difficulty of maintaining recreational organizations increased, a difficulty which cheap transport now available to nearby towns has accentuated.

What is to be done about it? What future is there for the traditional small English village community? What can the new science of planning do to maintain the beauty of the rural scene while satisfying, at the same time, the demand of the rising generation for the fuller life to which they are entitled, one which, rightly or wrongly, they think is available to them in greater abundance in the larger communities? For it is the young people and their future who must be the first consideration. The older folk are too close to the older convention into which they were born, and in which much of their lives has been passed, to feel the restlessness of the younger generation and its desire for a life more expansive than that which their villages can offer. There are 800 people, men, women, and children, in the village in which I live, with the normal proportion of boys and girls passing out from school each year. In the five years since the war I am not aware of any boy who has gone to work on the land, and only two have gone into work of any kind within the village; nor is the proportion of girls taking work in the place much higher. Agriculture and the few rural industries will do well if they can maintain the present level of the employment that they give; they have little to contribute to a 'Back to the Land' movement.

Not everyone realizes that country planning is as complex and difficult as town planning, though its problems are different. Superficial judgements, unsupported by experience, lead many people to become obsessed with the beauty of old buildings and peaceful scenes, without causing them to inquire what life must be in cottages often dilapidated, damp, and dark, however picturesque, without water-taps or sewage disposal, for people lacking most of the relaxations available even in the smallest towns. 'What a beautiful little place,' they say; 'I hope *they* won't do anything to spoil it.' However, this is no justification for despair. For those who will accept the need for change, there are various ways of attacking the problems which these places present. The most obvious is the repopulation of villages by the diffusion of industry. This can be done either by locating small industries in some of them, or by building larger ones in rural settings, and the deliberate planning of additional housing in the villages adjacent, to accommodate dormitory dwellers working in them. This is what is going on already in some places, and by either means the villages may regain an industrial element, the complement of the agricultural element in a balanced rural society, which they lost when the ancient rural crafts died out.

Of course, the problem of rural revival is not so simple as this. The introduction of a new industrial class into the old villages raises complex questions which will have to be answered. What proportion should it bear to the old society? How should the new housing be sited in relation to the old village, so that the whole may still remain one community? And so on. Then, too, there will be many small places in which this infiltration of a new industrial element cannot be contrived. In such cases, a scheme of grouping small places for many purposes may provide the way out. It is done already for administrative purposes through the District Councils and for primary education; the Free Churches have long been organized in this way, and the Established Church is tending more and more towards the union of benefices in sparsely populated parishes. The Cambridge Village Colleges have gone a long way to show what can be done to organize a fuller life for dwellers of all ages in the smaller rural communities on these lines, and there is scope for the application of experience and imagination in the further development of the principle.

Doubtless there are other village types which will call for still other forms of treatment if they are to provide the setting which modern youth demands. What is beyond any doubt is that we are working, at present, too much in the dark in our first efforts to plan the reorganization of rural life and labour. Planners themselves need to know far more of the history and the background of the country life which they are called upon to change and which they hope that their efforts may improve. Herein, I think, lies the great value of Mr Bonham-Carter's work. To a first-hand experience of country life in all its phases, and personal participation in local administration, he brings an appreciation of the value of history and tradition, an inquiring mind, a faculty for observation, and above all, a deep interest, entirely free from sentimentality, in the countryman and his environment. Thus, he has been led to reach back to the sources and origins of English rural society, to trace their evolution up to the present day, and so to provide both for himself and for others a body of facts and of evidence of human experience which should form a basis for a clearer judgement. That, I believe, is his main purpose in this book. It is not difficult, often, to see the directions in which his work is leading him, but in the main he has set out to provide his readers with a purely objective study of conditions of life in the English countryside, as the first step towards their reconstruction and development to meet the needs and aspirations of the countrymen and women of today.

PART ONE

The Background of Rural History

I

The Prehistoric Settlements

IT is generally considered that Britain became an island about 6000 B.C., by which time the great geological changes were nearly over. The immense glaciers of the Ice Age had finally retreated to the far north, the climate had turned warm and moist, the land had acquired a mantle of soil and vegetation, and the sea had closed over the fens, islands, and isthmuses that once connected Britain with the continent of Europe. About this time civilization was being born in the Near and Middle East, and primitive village communities were assembling in Asia Minor, in Egypt, and in the eastern Mediterranean. By contrast, man in Britain was still in the foetal stage. Some clues to his existence have come down to us – fragmentary human bones and rudimentary flint implements. He was certainly a hunter, and lived on wild animals, fish, and the fruits of the woods, but settlement proper did not exist.

Very slowly civilization spread northwards from the Mediterranean. Traders, prospectors, and peasants seeking fresh land pioneered the way. By 2500 B.C. Britain was receiving groups of colonists from western Europe who were acquainted with the essential arts of living. Many established themselves upon the chalk downs of the southern counties – vast stretches of scrub and turf, studded with flints, that rose above the swamps and forests in the valleys impenetrable below. Others populated the moorland areas of the south-west, and probed the entire Atlantic seaboard from Land's End to Cape Wrath. The Neolithic or New Stone Age had begun, so called after the characteristic use of stone for implements, an age in which change was as sudden and significant as that of almost any subsequent period in English history. At one stroke, as it were, human society took root and began to grow.

The principal innovation was a system of semi-nomadic agriculture, in which, for the first time, cropping played a significant part. Cultivation was confined to small plots of land, the soil stirred about with the hoe and the digging-stick, and a rough tilth obtained before the sowing of the seed. Wheat and barley were both grown, and when ripe were harvested with flint sickles. Livestock, however, was the main part of the economy, and included a species of small cow with long horns, sheep, goats, and pigs. Dogs had long been human companions. Thus diet was quickly altered from a monotony of coarse flesh and wild berries to a more balanced choice of meat, milk, cheese, and farinaceous cakes made from flour ground between two heavy stones. Pottery was familiar. Earthenware bowls and drinking-cups were in constant household use, and many were simply decorated and fitted with handles. There was a large variety of flint tools, but few weapons other than bows and arrows, for the settlers had small incentive for warfare; their chief enemy was the valley wolf, which preyed upon the stock. For protection, camps were founded upon the hill-tops and took the form of flat open spaces, fortified by concentric rings of ditches and banks. These were surmounted by timber palisades, and the camp itself was entered by a causeway that cut through a section of the earthwork. These were seasonal, not permanent, habitations, and places of emergency. To-day they are dry and waterless, and therefore totally unfit to live in, but four thousand years ago the climate was wetter and the water-table far higher than it is now. Thus sojourn, temporary at least,

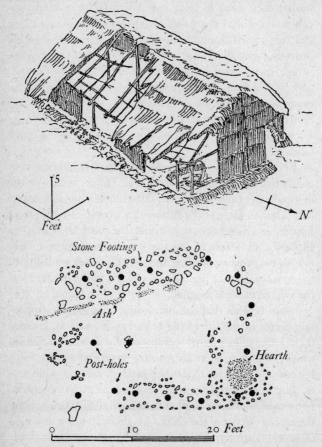

FIG. I. — *Plan and Isometric Reconstruction of Neolithic House at Haldon, Devon*

was quite possible for a group of families and their animals, and shelters of a rudimentary sort are known to have existed there. There is another impressive reminder of this early period in human history. The Neolithic peoples buried their dead in long mounds or barrows, and built cairns and burial chambers in honour of their chieftains. Practice varied. Long earth graves are a feature of inland districts, especially Wiltshire – a county with at least eighty such barrows. Megalithic tombs were confined for the most part to Cornwall, the Cotswolds, and the west coast. An exception, perhaps the most famous of all, was Wayland's Smithy, situated on the Berkshire Ridgeway near White-horse Hill; but the legend of Wayland belongs to a much later age.

The swarthy Mediterranean colonists were not the only distinctive Stone Age race in Britain. There were also the descendants of the aborigines, fair-complexioned probably, and known as 'the Peterborough people'. They were hunters and fishermen, frequenting the north and east, who adopted only a few of the southern improvements. Very few traces remain, but it is thought that they traded with the south, particularly in flint ware, and in the border areas the two races were mingled.

It can be seen that communication was soon an important factor in the life of the countryside. And so, because the chalk hills offered comparatively few obstacles to traffic, Wiltshire soon became the centre of an extensive system of downland roads that radiated far and wide, extending from south Devon to Kent and the eastern counties. Moreover, there was another reason why Wiltshire became the capital district of the south. About 1900 B.C. a new race of immigrants arrived, known as the Beaker folk (after the distinctive shape of their pottery), who prevailed over the southern natives. They were probably a more wholly nomadic people than the Stone Age farmers – owning cattle, little given to cultivation, and dwelling in tents and roughly roofed pits. They developed the use of metal, especially bronze (a compound of copper and tin, both mined in these islands), and they buried their dead in round, not long, barrows. At Avebury they constructed a magnificent temple composed of circles of immense sarsens, the whole area (about 28 acres) enclosed by a bank 35 feet high. (See Plate 2b.) The temple was approached by several avenues; that from West Kennett survives in part, is flanked by sarsens, and springs from a small circle on Overton Hill called 'the Sanctuary'. A short distance to the west stands Silbury Hill, a huge artificial mound over 100 feet high. It is solid, contains no tomb, and its significance is unknown. Besides these larger monuments there is a host of smaller ones, and of barrows, all in the same neighbourhood – a fact that emphasizes the importance of Avebury as a sacred centre. Twenty miles away near Amesbury stands Stonehenge, a smaller sanctuary, although hardly less impressive, and architecturally more remarkable. (See Plate 1a.) It was founded by the Beaker folk, then enlarged by their successors over the next five hundred years, and possibly adopted by the Celts and their priests, the Druids, in the millennium before Christ.

The existence of Avebury, Stonehenge, and the rest has important implications. The physical effort of collecting and raising the huge monumental stones (some came from as far away as Wales) implied a well-developed pattern of leadership and organization. There must have been uniformity of religion and a priesthood, and there must have been commerce and culture of an advanced order over a wide territory. However, it was not to last, and about 1500 B.C. a fresh wave of invasion from Brittany flowed over the south-west, absorbed the Beaker folk and profited from their improvements. These conquerors, who formed a new ruling class, were armed with the finest axes and daggers, all fashioned out of bronze. They had extensive trading connexions, importing amber from the Baltic, beads from the Mediterranean, and gold from Ireland; indeed gold now became the hallmark of luxury and was used lavishly by leading warriors and chieftains. Skilled smiths were installed, who specialized in bronze founding for the production of weapons, and in gold beating and engraving. Altogether society was demanding a larger number of specialists, and a higher, more civilized standard of living. The dead were still buried in round barrows, similar to but not identical with the Beaker type; and, in the course of time, it became the custom to burn the corpses and store the ashes in earthenware vessels. Avebury and Stonehenge, the latter enlarged, continued in full use, and the principal races – Neolithic, Beaker, and the newly established overlords – gradually fused into a composite people.

About 1000 B.C. small parties of Celtic refugees began to arrive in Britain from the Continent. The origins of this race are obscure, but it is likely to have arisen about the borders of Germany and France. In due course the Celts were pushed westwards by movements of other Germanic and east European stock, and thus Britain became their refuge. At first the immigrants settled down peaceably enough, but later, in the eighth century B.C., as the Continental pressure increased, they too invaded the south and the midlands in earnest and absorbed rather than displaced the indigenous inhabitants to whom they were already racially related. In their turn, the Celts brought important advances in agricultural and other techniques, but chiefly they introduced the fundamental conception of settled farming. The Celtic farm was at the same time a permeannt home, a place of work, and a fort. The steading was all contained within a stock fence or stockade, and consisted of a yard, thatched barns, byres, and dwellings, grain stores underground, and all the impedimenta of the farmer. The fields were small but regularly organized into square quarter-acre plots, each surrounded by a bank of stones or earth. The ground was tilled on a much more intensive scale than before. The hand hoe was replaced by a primitive plough drawn by oxen, but it is likely that this was still a scratching implement which merely stirred the earth without turning a true furrow. For this reason cultivation was still confined to the light upland soils, and although considerable progress was made towards clearing the lower slopes of the hills, the forests and heavy clays of the valleys remained unreclaimed and untouched. Nevertheless more food was being produced, and this made possible the higher population which immigration from the Continent was forcing upon the countryside. One limiting factor was the serious civil warfare that raged among the Celts, which accounts for the defended farms and other places of refuge. Even so, this was undoubtedly the foundation period of settled rural life, and while proper villages hardly existed as yet, the countryside was beginning to resolve itself into a pattern of isolated farms and hamlets. Such, for instance, was the case in the downland regions of southern England, where traces of many Celtic fields and settlements may still be detected. (See Plate 1b.)

Apart from agriculture, the Celts were notable for their industrial ability. Their bronze smiths were now a class apart, skilled independent craftsmen who travelled the countryside, working, and trading their goods. They manufactured in quantity craftsmen's tools such as chisels, punches, and tongs, household goods such as buckets and cauldrons, also ornaments and pins for personal decoration, and farm implements and weapons. But soon a development took place that affected not only the market for metal goods, but also methods of warfare and farm practice. This was the discovery of iron, first introduced into Britain about 450 B.C. At first change was slow, but very gradually the new metal displaced bronze in the manufacture of tools, arms, and goods in practical everyday use, although bronze was long retained for artistic and ornamental purposes. In agriculture, for instance, iron enabled Celtic farmers to expand and intensify their area of cultivation, and to venture deeper into the valleys. However, metal was not the only material symptom of a changing civilization. Pottery was similarly developed, for while the women continued to make rough pots for household use, craftsmen were soon turning out fine ware, both coloured and decorated, for ceremonial and festive occasions. Likewise, there were important advances in weaving and in other activities associated with the home. In addition, a lively trade existed with the Mediterranean; skins and metals were bartered for wine, and this in turn introduced a whole new range of drinking vessels of classical design, first aped, then metamorphosed by native artists into fine original work.

From such signs as these, and from the evidence of grave furniture and burial customs, it is clear that the Celtic village was an advanced and stratified community. This is strengthened by the remarkable discoveries at Meare and Glastonbury, Somerset lake villages dating from the second century B.C., situated in marshy, flooded ground, and constructed upon artificial foundations of logs, clay, and stones. At each village stood some sixty round thatched huts, with wattle walls and clay floors, and stone alleyways in between. Cattle were pastured and corn was grown on the higher land outside, while carts and canoes were the chief means of carriage. Hunting and wildfowling supplemented agriculture. Within the settlements flourished all the useful and some of the fine arts — woodwork, iron and bronze smithing, spinning, weaving, potting, and corn grinding by a new invention, the rotary hand quern. Even currency was in use, standard iron bars serving as coinage. Despite this evidence of civilized life, at no time did tribal warfare diminish. In fact, towards the end of the millennium it intensified. For this reason hill-top camps were widely developed both as fortresses and as tribal centres and rallying points — such places as Walbury Camp in south-west Berkshire, Cissbury near Worthing, and Maiden Castle (also, for a time, a permanent habitation) in Dorset. In Cornwall cliff castles fulfilled a similar function. However, it was in the south-east that the fiercest struggles developed and where, at the close of the prehistoric age, the greatest changes overtook the appearance of the countryside.

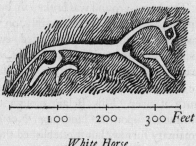

100   200   300 *Feet*

White Horse

2

The First Thousand Years A.D.

A FEW years before Julius Caesar's first expedition to Britain in 55 B.C. a new group of tribes had crossed the Channel from northern Gaul. These were the Belgae, a mixed Celtic-Germanic people, vigorous, bellicose, and adept in the uses of iron. They soon secured a large portion of the south-eastern counties – Sussex, Kent, Middlesex, Hertfordshire, and Essex – and with their axes they set about the clearance of the valleys and the felling of primeval forest. In due course they established iron industries in the Weald, and prepared much of the low-lying territory for cultivation. The heavy ground was broken up by a new and stronger type of plough, supported, possibly, on wheels and drawn by as many as eight oxen. It carried several of the fittings associated with the modern implement, which were wholly or partly made of iron – a coulter or knife to cut the turf, a share to undercut the sod, and an embryonic mould-board to turn it over. This Belgic plough exerted an important influence upon the landscape. Not only did it turn a rudimentary furrow, but it established the long narrow plot of the kind familiar to Norman and medieval farming. This method of cultivation, which existed contemporaneously with the small square fields on upland farms, was a great step forward in the exploitation of the soil; and it enabled the Belgae both to support themselves and to export grain to the Continent.

Belgic government and settlements were also relatively advanced. The capital was at Colchester, which had been developed as a port, and was, for a time, by far the most important place in the whole country. Belgic kings, including Cunobelin (Shakespeare's Cymbeline), issued coins in accordance with civilized custom. Indeed, during the entire period between the two main Roman invasions (54 B.C. and A.D. 43) a great deal was done to foster contact, commercial and cultural, between Britain and the Empire. No doubt this had a bearing on the decision taken by the Emperor Claudius to invade, for in economic terms, at least, the country had much to offer – land, metal, corn, timber, manpower. At all events, in A.D. 43, a large army was dispatched under Aulus Plautius, and within a few years secured not only the whole of the Belgic territory, but also most of England east of a line drawn from Devon to the Humber. In due course the frontier was pushed right forward under Agricola to the Scottish Highlands; later it was withdrawn and in A.D. 120 consolidated in the great stone wall built by Hadrian between Solway and the Tyneside. Within this boundary Roman Britain flourished for nearly two hundred and fifty years. Outside it, in Scotland, and in the wilder parts of Cornwall and Wales, lay the indigenous Britain of the Celts.

Once the conquest was assured, rapid progress was made towards a complete reorganization of the country. The old tribal areas were converted into provinces, and vast permanent roads laid down, with military units stationed at key points. At first powerful efforts were directed towards the creation of towns and town life, which to the Romans represented all that was best in civilization. By the end of the first century a number of important centres had come into existence, each with its distinctive Roman plan. Apart from London, by now the commercial and administrative capital, there were the veterans' colonies such as Gloucester and Lincoln, former tribal strongholds as at Winchester and Chichester, and garrison towns like Chester. Each of these possessed a wide range of amenities, of a type familiar to most citizens of the Empire, in particular a disproportionately large number of public buildings. A town of three or four thousand inhabitants, for instance, would be equipped with public baths, temples, and an amphitheatre for public games; also a town hall (capable of seating the entire population) sited on one side of a spacious market square. Naturally, trade was an important feature of town life, industries were established and no time was lost in exporting the main raw materials of the country, copper, tin, lead, gold, silver, iron, and coal. At the same time a variety of consumer goods, such as pottery and glass, were imported from abroad. Nevertheless, this did not alter the fact that the towns were largely an artificial creation, unable to support themselves, and dependent for their economic existence upon the countryside. Their chief justification lay in their function as centres of authority, and as practical examples of the Roman 'way of life'. However, early in the third century there was a marked decline in urban importance and prosperity. This was a phenomenon common to the entire Roman Empire, and was due to a variety of causes, of which one was fiscal. In Britain, at any rate, the underlying cause was the fundamental inability of the countryside to maintain an urban civilization, and in a comparatively short time a high proportion of the towns had materially and spiritually collapsed.

As a consequence many of the Romanized natives, who had constituted the majority of the town populations, withdrew into the countryside. There they extended the Roman system of landed property – the villa – which is known to have existed in Britain as early as the first century. Some of these villas were merely Celtic farmsteads rebuilt in the Roman fashion, but once the towns began to fall away there was a remarkable increase in the number of new and progressive estates that indicates a true rural prosperity. Normally a villa was a self-contained farm unconnected with any native village or settlement. As a general rule it consisted of a rectangular-shaped farmhouse with one or two wings, carefully sited on good soil or a protected slope. (See Fig. 2, below.) It was built of timber or brick, and contained eight or nine rooms dividing up the single storey. Fittings and decoration were in the familiar urban style — water from a well or by aqueduct, baths and central heating by hypocaust, frescoes on the walls, and tessellated floors.

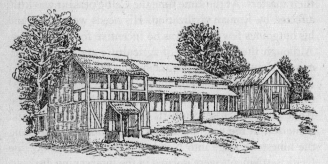

FIG. 2. — *The Roman Farm at Lockleys, Welwyn.*
Reconstruction after Excavation

In front of the house lay the farmyard, bounded by walls and by outbuildings such as stables, a barn with a threshing-floor, and labourers' quarters. The land was farmed on the Belgic system, that is, in long open plots and tilled with the *caruca*, the Belgic type of plough. Wheat was the staple crop, and the grain was sometimes dried over a furnace. Vines also were planted, and all the familiar domestic and farm animals were kept. As to crafts, there were carpenters and smiths to attend to all the normal requirements of the estate. Indeed, very little beyond metals and luxuries was needed from outside, and there was a wide range of home produce — bread, meat, milk, cheese, wine, wool, hides, timber, and many other things. By contrast, the native farming was unprogressive. The Celtic peasants, together with many of their animals, lived in round single-roomed huts roughly clustered into villages. Their farming was carried on as formerly in small square fields, ploughed with the primitive scratching implement, the *aratrum*; but it is not known whether they owned their land, or whether they held it on some system of tenure from Roman landlords. As a people they were pacific and relied upon the protection of their masters. At the same time the Celtic peasant was little affected by Roman civilization. His needs were small and his outgoings few; there was no incentive for assimilation. Although these two types of agriculture and rural society existed simultaneously, geographically they were separate. Most of the villas have been found close together in distinctive areas, round Bath and Winchester, in north-west Kent and west Sussex, in parts of Hampshire, Dorset, and Somerset, in the neighbourhood of Cirencester, and along the limestone ridge into Northampton and Lincoln. The Celtic settlements were isolated in the intervening districts, but in some of them — Cranborne Chase and the Fens, for example — it is considered that many of the villagers were employed on large imperial estates under Roman bailiffs.

Roman Britain did not die in a day, but once the Picts and Scots had finally broken through Hadrian's wall, and once the Saxon raiders had gained control of the North Sea, it declined very fast. By the end of the fourth century the situation was out of hand. The villas, although economically independent, were indefensible in the open countryside, and were gradually deserted. Serious revolts occurred among the peasants who shared in the general plunder and destruction. In 410 or soon after, all Roman troops and many officials were withdrawn, and the country was abandoned to its own resources. By 450 the nation had split up into a number of tribal states, and their mutual hostility contributed as much to the disorder as the barbarians. At length about the year 500 a warrior appeared who secured a transitory unity and gained some remarkable successes. Supposedly this was Arthur, a Roman Briton, and the last leader in the imperial tradition. He won a decisive victory over the Saxons in north-east Wiltshire, and comparative order was restored for the remainder of his lifetime. After his death, however, in 550 (due, legend says, to a private quarrel), the old Roman colonial society finally disintegrated in Britain.

Despite his successes, Arthur had never been able to do more than retard the progress of invasion, and ever since the middle of the fifth century settlements had been slowly but firmly established by one group of North German tribes after another: by the Jutes in Kent and the Isle of Wight; by the Saxons in many of the southern and home counties; and by the Angles who secured Norfolk, Suffolk, and in due course the whole of the north-eastern seaboard as far as the Scottish border. After 550 this process was accelerated, and by the middle of the seventh century the country had virtually been apportioned between the three principal states of Northumbria, Mercia, and Wessex. Thereafter until the ninth century history is concerned with the struggle between these three, and with the ultimate supremacy of Wessex. During this period the character of rural society underwent a profound change. The Anglo-Saxons consistently avoided the old centres of habitation. For superstitious reasons, perhaps, they allowed the ruined villa sites to disappear, and almost all the Roman towns to remain empty except for a handful of squatters. They were essentially gregarious, and wherever physical conditions permitted they lived together in large villages, situated for the most part on the lower ground, in direct contrast to the Celtic hamlets on the hills. Like the Belgae, but on a much larger scale, they were able to clear forests and exploit the richer soils of the valleys through their mastery of iron. The Saxon plough was of the heavy ox-drawn type, and tillage was mostly carried on in big unenclosed fields, subdivided into long narrow plots much like Belgic agriculture. In this way, for instance, the stiff clays and the thickly wooded Midland plains, hitherto unpopulated and untouched, were brought into cultivation. On the other hand, not all Anglo-Saxon England was so farmed. In the south-west and in the north large areas of wild land were reclaimed piecemeal through the efforts of individual settlers, living in lonely farmsteads. Even so the establishment of open field farming can be attributed to this period, and the framework of a system that was later elaborated into the manor. However, unlike Norman society, with its rigid and complicated pattern of relationships, the basis of the Anglo-Saxon village was the free peasants, linked by kinship, who owned their land and were subject to no man but the king. In fact, in comparative terms freedom was the hallmark of the early Anglo-Saxon community, in which social divisions were determined by a man's prowess and personality, and by the value of his *wergeld*, or blood money payable by his murderer. It is true that there were slaves, but these were drawn from subject races, in this case from those Celts and their descendants who had survived the invasions.

With certain exceptions (notably in Kent and in the Danelaw) landholding was reckoned in terms of the *hide*, an indefinite measure ranging from 40 to 120 acres of cultivable land. In general it was a balanced unit, calculated to support a family of substance, the actual size varying geographically, and in terms of the quality of the soil. Initially only a few obligations were attached to the ownership of property; none the less, they were serious — the supply of food to the king, the repair of bridges, and service in the army. However, as states evolved, a much larger list of duties was imposed upon the peasants and their communities. In addition the destructive internal wars and the later Danish invasions intensified the bare struggle for existence, and many small farmers were forced through starvation or the fear of it to apply to stronger and wealthier men for food and protection. This resulted in a gradual loss of freedom and in the growth of strict social hierarchies, in which a man of inferior status came to be loaded with obligations and restraints. One of the first stages in this process was the appointment by the king of a gesith or thegn to receive the food-rents formerly paid to himself by a particular village. Such payment was in kind, but later, owing perhaps to a series of bad harvests or a Danish raid, it was commuted for labour, since this was the one commodity that no disaster, other than wholesale extinction, could remove. In due course this arrangement was systematized, and a roster drawn up by which work was regularly performed on the thegn's land. This is merely one instance in which some of the features associated with the medieval manor were anticipated in the Anglo-Saxon village. By the Norman Conquest the thegn had reached a position in rural life equivalent to that of the lord of the manor. He dispensed private justice. His village property was extensive, several *hides* probably, and he held it in return for military service under the king. Likewise the geneat, the chief tenant of the thegn and in some sense a personal retainer who accompanied him on expeditions and fulfilled a number of important duties at home — escorting visitors, or carrying goods and messages. Next, the gebur, the most numerous of the landholders, who farmed a yardland or *virgate* (a quarter-hide, say 30 acres) or a *half-virgate* (15 acres) and who owned a pair of oxen. Below him stood the kotsetla, a true smallholder with 5 acres or so round his house, which he tilled with the spade. Technically all were regarded as free men. In fact the gebur and the kotsetla had many labour and other services to perform; freedom for them had virtually disappeared.

In the Danelaw – the Danish area of settlement, comprising East Anglia, Lincolnshire, Leicestershire, Nottinghamshire, and parts of neighbouring counties – the element of true freedom had survived much longer. Here the chief figure was the socman, an independent peasant proprietor, who paid his taxes direct to the king and performed a minimum of services to his immediate overlord. A different terminology was employed for land divisions: the *hide* was replaced by the *ploughland* or *carucate*, the acreage cultivable by an eight-ox plough team in a single year; each *ploughland* being sub-divided into eight *ox-gangs* or *bovates*. However, the open field system was followed in much the same manner as in the rest of England, although the individual holdings tended to be smaller, owing possibly to the practice of splitting up the land on inheritance. After the Conquest much of the Danelaw was feudalized, but in a few counties the socman was permitted to retain many of his privileges.

In substance, therefore, there were many similarities between the Danish and the Saxon civilizations. In the countryside the ox, an improved breed, was the main support of a co-operative agriculture. In the farmsteads animals and human beings were quartered under the same roof in a large barn-like building. So far as possible each village was a self-contained economic and social unit. Herein lay the motive prompting all the regulations that governed both farm practice and rural society – regulations formulated by the Normans into a tight legal code, within which the strains and stresses of village life were actively at work from Domesday until the Black Death.

3

The Manor

FOR the first few years following the Conquest, the Normans were busy strengthening their hold upon the countryside. William I divided up the native estates among his friends and supporters, to the extent that hardly a single Saxon thegn was left in possession of his own land. Furthermore, the feudal system of allegiance introduced by William, although similar to both Saxon and Continental organization, was entirely centralized and much more rigorous than either. As a result the king, the nominal source of all power, was in an unrivalled position to enforce authority. In the English countryside, feudalism had the effect not only of substituting Norman for Saxon property owners, but also of degrading many of the free tenants into a new unfree class who were tied far more closely to the soil. The following simplified table sets out the chief ranks of Saxon and Norman society from which approximate comparisons can be made.

SAXON	*Status*	NORMAN
Thegn	Overlord	Baron
Geneat		Freeman
or ⎬ Free Tenants		Socman
Socman		Villein
Gebur	Unfree Tenants	Bordar
Kotsetla		Cottar
Theow	Slave	Serf

In 1085 William decided, for purposes of information and taxation, to make a survey of the whole country. By the following year the task was complete and the findings published in Latin in Domesday Book. This was a collection of basic facts, gathered by royal commissioners who had visited each village and estate and interrogated the chief inhabitants. The scope of the survey may be summarized as follows:

(1) The name and extent of the manor.

(2) The owner of the manor (a) in King Edward the Confessor's time; (b) in 1085–6.

(3) The number of tenants; their status, and the size of their holdings.

(4) The quantity of wood, meadow, pasture, and arable ground.

(5) The number of plough teams.

(6) The number of mills, quarries, and fisheries.

(7) The quantity and variety of livestock.

(8) The value of the manor (a) in King Edward the Confessor's time; (b) when bestowed by King William after the Conquest; (c) in 1085–6.

Not many of the reports answer *all* these inquiries, but the following two extracts from Domesday, referring to manors in different parts of the country, will give an impression of the type of information provided.

BERKSHIRE
LIST OF THE KING'S PROPERTIES

In Chenetberie (Kintbury) Hundred

The King holds Chenetberie in demesne. King Edward held it. There are 2 hides. There is land for 10 ploughs. On the demesne are 2 ploughs; and (there are) 15 villeins and 16 bordars with 8 ploughs. There are 2 serfs and 2 mills worth 32 shillings and 6 pence; and 40 acres of meadow, and woodland to render 3 swine. In King Edward's time, as afterwards and now, it was worth 10 pounds. Henry de Ferrers holds of this manor 43 acres of land which were in the King's ferm in King Edward's time according to the testimony of the shire (moot). They state also that the sheriff Godric made this into pasture land for his own horses; but by what warrant they do not know.*

NOTTINGHAMSHIRE

THE LAND BELONGING TO GEOFFREY ALSELIN

In Laxintune (Laxton) Tochi had 2 carucates of land (assessed) to the geld. (There is) land for 6 ploughs. There Walter, a man of Geoffrey Alselin's, has 1 plough and 22 villeins and 7 bordars having 5 ploughs and 5 serfs and 1 female serf and 40 acres of meadow. Wood (land) for pannage 1 league in length and half a league in breadth. In King Edward's time it was worth 9 pounds; now (it is worth) 6 pounds.†

Domesday Book gave William invaluable insight into the state of the nation. It told him, for instance, that the disturbances caused by the Conquest and subsequent repressions had had to be paid for by lower land values and by a reduced human and stock population. It also furnishes posterity with a very fair idea of the appearance and substance of early feudal villages, which together constituted the wealth and being of the country as a whole. The following description is imaginary, but it might well have applied to any part of the south Midlands during the twelfth century. Elsewhere, especially in the north and west, there were considerable variations.

The village was reached by a rough track, rutted and patched with stones, beside which there straggled twenty or thirty dwellings. Some were mere hovels. Others, at best, were single-storey cottages, built of a hard grey chalk called *clunch*, studded with flints, or of a rude timber framework

---

* William appropriated direct many of the Saxon royal manors and properties. Godric was sheriff of Berkshire before the Conquest, but fell at the battle of Hastings. 'Demesne' and 'ferm' mean, in this instance, royal property.

† 'Geld' was a land tax originating from the Danegeld. 'Pannage' means the right to graze pigs.

with walls of wattle and daub. The roofs were thatched, and the interiors consisted of one or perhaps two rough rooms, inhabited by a peasant family together with its pigs and poultry. The church, a more substantial building, was on a rise and boasted a small wooden tower. The priest lived nearby, either in a cottage, or, if he was fortunate, in a superior dwelling provided for him by a pious benefactor, or by a religious house in the neighbourhood. The lord of the manor, a baron, lived a small space apart from the village, either in a castle or in a fortified manor house. This was an imposing building of stone, containing a large central hall but no chimneys, and was sited with its attendant barns and stables in the middle of the demesne or home farm. As for the remainder of the land, this was divided into garden plots attached to each cottage; into smallholdings or crofts of five or six acres farmed by individual tenants; and into the big open fields and meadows, several hundred acres in extent, that were tilled and grazed in common. Ideally all the land on the manor was allotted for use according to the nature and value of the soil. Thus meadows for hay and pasture were set aside from low-lying land near a stream, arable from the plain or nether slopes of the hills where the ground was easily worked, and rough grazing from downland or heath; the rest was forest or waste. In principle every peasant had access to every kind of land, but the size of the holding and the common rights varied according to a man's status and resources.

There were usually three (sometimes two, sometimes four) open arable fields in a manor; thus the crop rotation followed was three-course – wheat or rye in the west field (to provide bread for the community); barley in the east (from which ale was brewed without hops; a common average of consumption was a gallon per man per day); alternatively oats, peas, or beans might be sown for winter fodder. The third field, exhausted from the corn crops of the two previous years, lay fallow, was dunged and grazed by stock all winter, and partially cleaned of weeds by several ploughings in spring, summer, and autumn. Thus each field would bear crops for two years and rest the third – a crude, wasteful system that gradually depleted the resources of the land.

For purposes of cultivation, each field was divided up into strips. Theoretically each strip was 22 yards wide

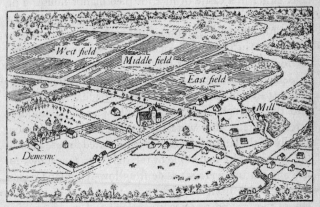

FIG. 3. – *A Medieval Village*

(about four poles) and 220 yards long (a furrow-long or furlong, the distance an ox-team could plough without a rest): thus one acre in all, which was reckoned the amount of land ploughable by oxen in a single day, although the actual quantity was probably less than this. The strips often varied in size and shape, dependent upon the nature of the land. They were probably formed by ploughing two furrows, one up and one down, in the centre of the strip. These two furrows would fall against each other and cover a narrow line of unploughed turf. The remainder of the strip would then be ploughed out, with the result that in the course of time a high bank or baulk would be built up in the centre, and deep open furrows would be excavated on the outer sides of the strip. These open furrows would act as boundaries and as drains for carrying away surface water. Some authorities say the *baulks* were the boundaries, and this may have been so if two neighbours had thrown up a ridge against each other on the outside edge of their strips, which would have left the water-furrows in the centre.* In addition, when strips lay on a hill, ploughing was done laterally and the furrows turned downhill; this caused the

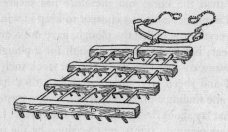

FIG. 4. – *Medieval Farm Implements – Harrow*

soil to slip, and in time it piled up into a baulk (known in this case as a *lynchett*) and resulted in a terrace formation. At the end of each strip was the headland or turning-place of the plough team, and this was ploughed last, or left as a grass drove. Fencing was plainly impossible between strips, and unnecessary, but entire open fields sown with crops were fenced, each man providing hurdles, posts, or brush-wood along that part where his land adjoined the perimeter of the field; and fines were rightly heavy if such work was neglected and cattle strayed on to the corn.

* There is still considerable speculation on this subject. See *English Husbandry,* by Robert Trow-Smith (Faber), and *A History of English Farming,* by C. S. Orwin (Nelson).

In summer most animals were turned out together on to the stubbles, or grazed at liberty over the commons, or stinted, that is, restricted by number, on meadows where grazing was controlled. Such were the hay meadows which, until the crop was mown and gathered in, were fenced and apportioned to individual farmers; thereafter they were stocked. Stockmen paid by the village looked after the different herds – cattle, sheep, or pigs. Since root crops were unknown, few cattle survived the winter, and a large proportion had to be slaughtered in the autumn and the carcasses salted down. The ox was a prized possession. It was quieter than the horse and therefore less severe on the wooden implements; it was cheaper to keep in winter, and it did everything – pulled the plough, gave milk, and made good meat; but few men had enough for a plough team, which was a co-operative effort. Other stock such as pigs, poultry, and sheep were prized less, but they had their place, some finding a precarious living on the wasteland or forest that lay about the boundaries of the village. Here too there were common rights, much valued by the peasants, and essential to the economy of the village: the right to small wood and turf for fuel, to furze and reed for thatching, besides the illegal but no less popular practice of snaring. By modern standards crop yields were poor. Two bushels per acre of wheat and rye produced ten bushels, and four bushels of oats and barley brought in twelve to sixteen bushels, say about one-quarter of the yields expected to-day. This is not surprising in view of the primitive and exhausting rotations practised, of the crude implements that could only disturb the top spit of the soil, of the utter lack of deep drainage, of the absence of manures other than dung, and of the general inability to improve farming methods, since all must suffer if one man failed to play his part.

In property matters there was a strong affinity with the

past. In theory all land belonged to the king, the barons holding their estates under the crown in return for military service. In the same way all village farmers, free or unfree, held their lands on tenure from the lord of the manor in return for certain services. These services varied and their variety largely determined the status of the farmer. Thus a villein, who might rent as many as thirty strips (a virgate) in the open fields, had to fold his sheep on his lord's land, and work several days a week (week work) and all harvest days as well (boon work) on the demesne, providing his own implements and oxen. In a similar position were the bordar, who had fewer strips, and the cottar, who had no land at all outside his cottage garden and paddock, both of whom supplemented their living by doing piece or day work for others. In addition to services, produce rents were demanded and paid in corn and honey, the latter providing wax for candles and ointment, sugar, and mead – a popular alcoholic drink. In a more prosperous class were the freeman and the socman, who had fewer or no labour services to perform, but who supplied the manpower for military expeditions. There were many other obligations. A bondman (or unfree tenant) could not sell or dispose of his land in any way, and at his death his son had to pay a fine to ensure succession. Similarly fines were levied for the marriage of a daughter, for apprenticeship, and for many business transactions. A free tenant was subject to none of these restraints. He could sell his land at will, and his son inherited it without payment. He could fold his sheep on his own ground and he could sue his lord in the king's court where the bondman had no redress at all. On the other hand, all were obliged to take their corn to the lord's mill, and all had to suffer the depredations of his pigeons.

Another obligation was attendance at the Manor Court. This was held monthly, or at longer intervals, in the hall of the manor house, in the church, or in the centre of the village under a great tree. Although virtually controlled by the lord of the manor, it was democratically constituted with a jury of tenants, elected every year, under the chairmanship of the steward, the lord's representative. Its duties were manifold. They included keeping the rolls or records wherein were stated the exact nature of each tenancy, the condition of the fields and the value of the estate; fixing and maintaining rules for good farm practice; enforcing all the fines and penalties and administering petty justice; annually appointing all the parish officials (e.g. the *reeve*, an overseer who also represented the village interests; the *hayward*, who looked after the fences; the *woodward*, who was concerned with the forest or waste; the *shepherd*, the *ox-herd*, the *swineherd*, etc.). In this way was built up a body of village law, known as the 'custom of the manor', which it became ever harder, even for the lord, to override, or from which to deviate at all without the general consent of the village.

As for the lord himself, in early days he divided his time between hunting and fighting. And if he was a man of substance owning several properties, he moved about with numerous retainers from one manor to another, eating up the provisions that had been accumulated against his arrival. In his absence his place was taken by the steward, or by the bailiff, the medieval equivalent of a factor. Much estate business, however, devolved upon the reeve, a bondman, whose duty it was to see that all the daily work was done, and who attended to the accounts. A certain number of farm servants and specialists were also employed on the demesne, and their work was additional to the labour services rendered by the tenants. These men were paid wages, in money and in kind, and some of them were appointed by the manorial court. Finally there were the craftsmen, who, in so far as they had cottages and a little land, were liable for service like the rest. This they performed through the medium of their callings – masons, smiths, carpenters, potters, shoe and harness makers, basket-makers, and the like. The miller also was an important figure, for the mill was the lord's monopoly.

Such was the internal economy of the village, which was practically self-supporting. Imports were few and were restricted to the absolute essentials – iron and steel for the ploughs, scythes, sickles, and ox- or horse-shoes, spices and salt for seasoning, mill stones, brass or copper pots, tar for

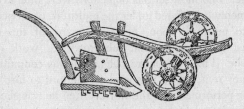

FIG. 5. – *Medieval Farm Implements–Plough*

sheep scab; no doubt a few luxuries were also obtained for the lord's household. All this was bartered or paid for by the sale of surplus corn, wool, and hides, or of the products of the craftsmen, at the nearest market or fair. The market was generally a local affair held, as nowadays, at frequent intervals, weekly or monthly. But the fair was on a much larger scale and an annual event. There were only two mentioned in Domesday, but the number increased as the centuries passed. One of the best known in the south was St Giles' Fair at Winchester. This was held for sixteen days between 31 August and 15 September and had been granted by royal charter to the Bishop of Winchester. Entrance fees were charged, and dues had to be paid on every transaction, also rent for the stalls. On the other hand, goods were generally cheaper than in local markets and of a far greater variety, for merchants came from far and wide, even from abroad. And while the Fair was on, all other trade in the area was forbidden; thus the attendance was enormous and business well worth while.

The feudal system, so far as it affected the village, worked well enough for two and a half centuries, from 1100 to 1350. At its best it offered absolute security and tolerable conditions of life. At its worst it was rigid and repressive. Indeed this element of rigidity contributed to its decline, for the system was unable to absorb profound economic change. The most serious objections were offered by the bondmen who suffered under the multitude of services they had to perform. Soon, however, many of the villeins secured the right to find substitutes for work on the demesne. Then the entire obligation was commuted for a money rent, which was used by the lord to hire labour for the performance of the work. Often he was glad to do this, for it had become ever harder to extract a full day's work from the tenants. By the early 1300s commutation of services was common, and, although the lord retained the right to revert to the old system, there was rarely any going back. Another change was put in hand by the lord himself, and it was not a popular one. Where labour was scarce, he took to letting off the demesne in one or more separate farms, receiving a rent in exchange. This often proved a better investment than managing his own home farm, and consequently there was a tendency towards yet another innovation – enclosure. Not only did the lord begin to enclose the demesne where possible, but he also extended it by taking in part of the common waste. This aroused strong opposition, for it deprived the peasants of an important part of their living – the right to turn small stock out to forage, and to gather fuel, house timber, and thatching materials. Also commercial enterprise at the expense of the community was deprecated by the church, and in 1236 the Statute of Merton was passed to control or forbid these ventures.

However, as yet none of these changes was sufficiently sudden or rude to disturb the surface of country life. That there was real prosperity at times, especially during the early part of the twelfth century, is evidenced by the sustained burst of ecclesiastical building, when nearly all the parish churches were built or rebuilt in timber and stone. In 1348, however, the country was assailed by the Black Death, which in two years reduced the population by a third, possibly by a half. All over the countryside land lay untilled, cottages and hamlets deserted. The price of labour quickly rose by fifty per cent, and this had a threefold effect. It made the lord chary of commuting further services, and in some cases the process was reversed, for labour, even for hire, was hard to come by. In some instances land had to be sold freehold, for no man could be found to work it or tenant to rent it. Secondly, it made life difficult for the small farmer in that, while the rent remained constant, his household and family — his earning power — had been halved by disease. Lastly, it put the labourer in a position to bargain for better wages and conditions. Of this he took full advantage, and many broke the rules of the manor, left home and found work with any employer who would pay more. Parliament then stepped in and from 1349 onwards passed a series of 'Statutes of Labourers', designed to freeze wages and restore economic order. Gradually conditions were tightened up and desperate attempts were made to restore the former stability. All hired persons were ordered to work upon the land at the place where they lived and at the rates paid in 1346. Only if no work was available might they move to another manor. Yet in spite of this the drift to the towns went on. Penalties made little difference, for statute after statute was passed. At the same time Justices of the Peace were appointed by the Crown to assess wages locally and to enforce the laws passed. Ironically enough, the appointment of these officers further reduced the authority of the manor, for wage-fixing had hitherto been one of the main functions of the Manor Court.

In 1381 matters came to a head, and nation-wide disturbances broke out, known as the Peasants' Revolt. The peasants wanted the abolition of villeinage and of manorial dues and restraints, land to be let at a perpetual rent of fourpence an acre, and free buying and selling. After preliminary success, the revolt was defeated; nevertheless the chief demands were all satisfactorily obtained during the following century, partly, no doubt, as a result of the violence, and partly as the outcome of economic change. The integrity of the feudal manor had, therefore, been largely destroyed by the end of the fourteenth century, but the manor itself did not disappear. It could not; its nature merely altered. The feudal lord gradually turned himself into a commercial landlord. He continued the practice of leasing the demesne, bought back his freeholds at every opportunity and rented them out again. He also converted unfree tenure into freehold of a sort, whereby the villein became a 'copyholder', paying a money rent for his land, the title to which was a copy of the Manor Court Roll. Between 1350 and 1450 rural society altered greatly. There was a great increase in individual freedom; but by cutting the bonds that bound them to the land, the peasant and the labourer laid themselves open to the fluctuations of capital enterprise, and in due course this caused them far greater sorrow than the hardships of the feudal manor.

4

The Growth and Influence of Commercial Farming

In the early days of the manor, money was a rarity for the peasant, since by means of barter and personal labour he had been able to a large degree to dispense with it altogether. However, as time went on, cash became essential both for the payment of feudal dues and for the conversion of services into rent. Likewise, it was needed by the larger tenant and freehold farmers, and by the landlord, to buy the materials and hire the labour which had previously been obtained by feudal means. This was the primary cause of the tremendous development in sheep farming between 1350 and 1550, for sheep and pasture required less expenditure than arable farming, and they showed far higher returns. In due course – apart from temporary setbacks in the late fourteenth and early fifteenth centuries – sheep became so popular that the profit motive entirely replaced what had at first been merely an expedient to save labour and make ends meet. This encouraged the larger landholders to commercialize their estates and enclose demesne and common land on an even larger scale than before. In this way huge sheep walks were created, especially in the West Country, in the Midland and Eastern Counties, and in west Yorkshire, and flocks rapidly increased – at one time there were reckoned to be as many as 150,000 sheep on the manors in East Anglia alone. Even among the small men sheep increased at the expense of tillage and other livestock. The open fields were deteriorating under the continuous corn cycle, and yields were so low that harvest barely sufficed to feed the country at large. For a peasant the small surplus available for sale was not enough; therefore he too tried to consolidate his strips and convert at least some of his arable into pasture.

The immediate repercussions of these changes were widespread and severe. Not only did the loss of land and rights bear hardly on the villager, but in some counties (Warwickshire, for example) hamlets and whole villages were swept away to make room for the shepherd and his dog. As a consequence there were loud protests from all sides and outbreaks of violence, but on this occasion the rioters had official support. Led, sometimes by prominent men, at others by their manor officers, groups of peasants on whose territory the sheep had encroached sallied out to tear down the fences and scatter the flocks. Enclosure was repeatedly forbidden by Parliament, but with little avail. It is estimated that by 1550 half a million acres of arable land had been lost to pasture, and some fifty thousand people put out of business by the sheep enclosures. The fact was that wool paid, and in pastoral areas farming was fast becoming a capitalist enterprise. It was here that the new class of yeoman farmer made his mark; and it was his economic freedom that engendered new conceptions of social liberty.

The wool trade, with which these changes in farm practice were intimately associated, had long been of national importance. At first the raw material had been exported in large quantities to Flanders for manufacture – long wool from the valley breeds for worsteds and serges, short wool from the hill breeds for cloth. After the accession of Edward III in 1327 this policy was altered. With the aid of Flemish immigrants a native clothmaking industry was established that by the sixteenth century had secured first place in the export trade, and in due course absorbed practically the entire output of home-grown wool. In either case sheep farming was stimulated, and in several parts of the country the prosperity of the times is still reflected in the nobility and beauty of the villages, with their fine churches and monuments, strong serene houses, and ample market places and halls; notable examples are Chipping Campden in Gloucestershire, a famous wool centre, and the cloth villages of Coggeshall in Essex and Lavenham in Suffolk. Late in the sixteenth century the impetus of the wool trade was reduced, and once more farming and the general pattern of the countryside began perceptibly to alter.

This, the Elizabethan era, is rightly regarded by historians as one of material and mental prosperity. It is best remembered nowadays by the magnificence of the country mansions, which the National Trust is hastening to preserve; by the charm and solidity of the farmhouses built by the new class of freeholder or yeoman; by the colleges of Oxford and Cambridge; by the flowering of the arts which yielded the madrigal composers, the miniaturists, and the writers such as Spenser, Sidney, Shakespeare, Marlowe, Ben Jonson. Trade, too, expanded in every direction, at home and overseas, and London grew great in size and importance. For the first time for two hundred years the population began to rise, and food soon became a matter of great concern to this vigorous and prolific nation. The demand for corn gradually improved, and wheat rose from less than 5s. a quarter in 1500 to nearly 40s. in 1600. In addition, Parliament took more effective steps both to penalize sheep enclosure and to subsidize the arable farmer. Mixed farming regained its balance, and corn benefited from the fact that the land, after a century of grass, responded miraculously. The long rest, and the treading and dunging of the sheep restored heart to the soil, and yields practically doubled.

How, then, fared the villager at this time, say in the year

1600? At the bottom of the scale stood the landless labourer, the descendant of the cottar and the serf, who lived almost entirely on his wages. If housed by his employer, he was probably better off than if he lived out. He was sure of food and lodging, was accepted by the household and earned £2 or £3 a year. A skilled man, e.g. a stockman, earned a little more and had a few privileges besides. Wages were fixed, not by the farmers, but by the Justices of the Peace in each county, and rates for workers who lived on their own were about double those for workers who lived in. Day rates were higher still and varied, according to the locality and the season, from 3d. to 1s. Low as these rates may seem, they compared favourably with Continental standards of the time, and they enabled a countryman and his family to live adequately in an average year. In bad times, however, they were not enough. The labourer with little or no land was the first to suffer, and it was he who formed the bulk of the beggars who roamed the countryside. On the other hand, farm servants, as a class, were by no means settled in their station. Many saved enough money to start farming on their own, either by renting or buying a smallholding, or by squatting – that is, reclaiming a piece of wasteland. In later years lack of proper title made the squatters' position precarious, and they were never popular with the village. Nevertheless, the labourer without land was still in the minority, and it was not until the Great Enclosures of the late eighteenth and early nineteenth centuries that there appeared a large, permanent, and depressed class of landless countrymen, who were absolutely dependent on their wages and on the farmers who paid them.

Next in the rural hierarchy stood the smallholder with a cottage and five, ten, or twenty acres of land, of which he was often the owner, and with the usual rights over the commons. His status and his existence were similar to the labourer's in that he had to supplement his living by working for his neighbours, but he always retained a measure of independence by virtue of his holding. Above him stood the yeoman, who was either a freeholder or a copyholder, with land still parcelled out among the open fields or recently enclosed by voluntary agreement. Already there were examples of yeomen farming several hundred acres and living like gentry, but perhaps a farm of between fifty and a hundred acres was an average size, worked by the farmer and his family and one or two hired labourers. The copyholder was no different from the freeholder in this matter, but the former was a tenant paying a money rent and his son would have to meet a premium on inheritance. In addition, there were other farmers who held their land on lease for a term of years, or temporarily at the will of the landlord.

In appearance the village remained much the same as of old, although there were a few changes. The yeomen, for instance, lived in what appear to modern eyes as cottages, but were in fact small farmhouses, built of timber, brick, stone, or other local material. The labourers had their cabins, reconstructed, perhaps, but still rudimentary. Farming was very little advanced. Open fields and commons still predominated, cultivation was hide-bound and primitive, few cattle were allowed to survive the winter, and there was an immense expanse of wood and waste. As to food, although some fared better than others, the quantity and variety of meat, corn, and greenstuff depended entirely on the success of the current season or previous harvest. Storage and preservation were the great stumblingblocks to plenty, while a bad harvest brought actual starvation. Fresh meat was exceptional, eaten only on feast days or at the slaughter of stock when the summer grazing was over. Game could generally be had, legally or otherwise, in the winter months, especially pigeons, which were bred in large numbers on the great estates; all else was salted down and stored. Often the poor man could not afford to eat his own pig meat, poultry, or eggs, but sold them for ready cash; likewise butter, cheese, and milk. In the ordinary way he fed his family on messes of porridge and skimmed milk with maslin (a coarse bread made of barley and rye, or if times were bad of beans and peas mixed in with the flour). Wheaten bread was a luxury found only in the better houses. Vegetables and salads, such as turnips, carrots, cabbage, lettuce, cucumber, and a few herbs, were available in a small way; but potatoes were a later innovation and did not gain in popularity for many years. Fish, fresh or salted, was another standby and, for other than religious reasons, was widely eaten in Lent when the stock of winter meat was getting low. Fruit was also grown in cottage gardens and orchards. This was the source of many home-made wines, besides cider, perry, a light beer brewed from barley, and honey drinks. Such was the repertory of the farmhouse and the cottage.

It is clear that by 1600 the countryside had outgrown the chrysalis of feudalism, although rural society was far from solving the problems of the new age. Among these the greatest, undoubtedly, was poverty. Who, then, were the poor? In the sense that a man with few possessions was poor, the problem was no worse in the sixteenth century than in any other. In feudal times each man had had a place in society from which it was difficult to escape, even had he wished. In Elizabethan times he was free, theoretically, to earn his own living. In practice he was often destitute, having neither duties towards nor support from those in authority. For most of the century the poor were left to their own fate. This sudden change in attitude was due not only to the disintegration of the manor, but also to the dissolution of the monasteries, great charitable harbours of the needy, and to the disastrous end of the Hundred Years' War with France, when numbers of ex-soldiers and feudal retainers were thrown upon the labour market. In due course bands of unemployed, unwanted and desperate men began to rove the countryside, robbing, and generally resorting to crime for their living. 'The beggars' became a byword – the enemies of the village, and the terror of the towns. Few realized that this poverty was the product of the system and of the times, and that to be out of work was not necessarily the fault of the individual. At first some relief was afforded, at any rate in the towns, in a number of different ways – by cheap or free food, by child welfare, and by loans to business. A few hospitals were founded to look after the sick, the orphans, and the lunatics, the money provided by private charity. These efforts, admirable in themselves, were only piecemeal and therefore could never be wholly satisfactory. When Parliament began at last to take notice of the problem, official action was restricted to repression. Penalties, often savage ones, were imposed for unlicensed begging, and special gaols (with the hard title of 'houses of correction') were set up in every county, where 'sturdy' (i.e. able-bodied) vagabonds were put to work. Later a more humane attitude was adopted, slum clearance was ordered, and efforts were made to secure a cottage and four acres of land for every countryman with a family. However, little of this legislation took effect: it was altogether too primitive and experimental.

At length in 1597 was passed the first comprehensive Poor Law, confirmed in 1601, the foundation of all subsequent Acts, laying down principles that virtually held good until the early nineteenth century. Its outstanding provision was to make the parish (the church unit of government) the executive body for all poor law administration, while detailed responsibility was placed upon the shoulders of the churchwardens and new officials called overseers, who acted under the general supervision of the Justices of the Peace. Their duties (which will be further described in Part Two) comprised the care of all poor persons, whatever the cause of their poverty – sickness, old age, unemployment, lawlessness – and whatever may be said about poor law administration in later years, there is no doubt that these measures were initially successful. The army of 'sturdy vagabonds' was disciplined and reduced, and the worst cases of poverty were relieved. In addition, from this time forward, nearly every parish was accumulating a stock of useful charities – sums of money or bequests of land left by private individuals for the purchase of coal, bread, or medical comforts for the benefit of the poor. Rural poverty, however, remained an intractable problem, and it was to loom even larger in the subsequent history of the countryside.

5

The Agrarian Revolution

I N spite of social problems, there was promise of great agricultural progress in the early years of the seventeenth century. Although wholesale enclosure had been restrained, the enclosing movement steadily continued, and took the form of mutual arrangements between village farmers who wished to consolidate their holdings. By this time it was beginning to be realized that enclosure was indispensable to any improvement in farming technique, and a number of writers – some sensible, others merely extravagant – were already pointing the way forward. Agricultural literature was, of course, nothing new. During the previous century some admirable textbooks had appeared, notably in 1523 Fitzherbert's *Boke of Husbandrye* and *Boke of Surveyinge and Improvements*; the former a practical work about farming in the Derbyshire Peak District, the latter among other things a guide to the relations between landlord and tenant. Perhaps the best-known Elizabethan agricultural writer was Thomas Tusser, whose *Hundreth Good Pointes of Husbandrie* was published in verse in 1557, later expanded into *Five Hundreth Good Pointes of Husbandrie, united to as many Good Pointes of Huswifery*. Like several of his successors (Arthur Young, for example) Tusser failed as a farmer, but his book, although not revolutionary, was full of wise saws and useful suggestions, and incidentally painted a faithful portrait of contemporary country life. It has been reprinted many times. Another valuable book was Barnaby Googe's *Foure Bookes of Husbandrie*, a translation from the German, which contained much helpful information about the Low Countries, where there was then, as now, an advanced type of agriculture. At the turn of the century the list increases. There was Leonard Mascall on cattle, Sir Hugh Plat on manuring and sowing (he advocated dibbling corn), Gervase Markham, a hack who wrote about practically anything, John Gerard the herbalist, Rowland Vaughan on meadow drowning, Charles Butler and John Levett on bees. Later we hear of Gabriel Plattes, a writer and an inventor who took out a patent for a corn drill, Samuel Hartlib, an unscrupulous publisher who pretended to the authorship of a number of works on agriculture, Walter Blith, a strict Puritan and a pioneer in field drainage, and John Worlidge, a prolific writer and inventor, who anticipated several of the improvements associated with the following century.

Despite this flood of serious literature and the intense interest that must have existed, very little practical progress was made. Few of the writers were farmers, and most practising farmers were either hamstrung by the open fields or mentally too limited to alter their ways. Besides this the Civil War did much to discourage agricultural enterprise, more through a sense of insecurity than by any destruction caused, and even after the Restoration the situation did not quickly recover. The only important exception was the reclamation of a large part of the East Anglian fens under the direction of Cornelius Vermuyden. Nevertheless the seeds of progress were surely being sown, and in the matter of crop rotation the pioneer work was already being performed by Sir Richard Weston, a Royalist gentleman who had taken refuge in Holland during the troubles. There he had noted the practice of growing turnips for winter fodder and clover for hay, and after his return to England he experimented with both these crops on his farm in Surrey, and left his observations for publication. However, his example was not immediately followed, for reasons already explained. For one thing, according to the custom of the manor, all livestock were permitted to graze the stubbles and fallows from August till February; thus winter cropping was impossible. In addition, farmers were reluctant to improve their land, for without tenant right they were merely benefiting the landlord and increasing their own rent. Therefore it was only on freehold and enclosed farms that tests could be made, and crops other than the traditional attempted at all. On the other hand, the advantages were enormous. Both clover and turnips were late sown in the fallow field, after a thorough cleaning and working down of the soil. Clover and newly-sown grasses yielded more hay and grazing, and of a far higher quality than could ever be obtained from the manorial pastures, and when ploughed in, the sward enriched the soil with the humus that was so necessary for the corn crops to follow. Turnips also induced fertility through dunging and treading, and enabled sheep and cattle to survive the winter.

Progress in cropping was only one part of the story. Soon a similar advance was being made in the design and use of implements, in particular the drill and the horse hoe. These two implements, although not entirely original, were substantially the invention of Jethro Tull, a Berkshire farmer, born and buried at Basildon, a small village about eight miles north-west of Reading. All his experiments, however, were carried out on two farms on the borders of the county. In his book *Horse-hoeing Husbandry*, published in 1733, he explains how, on his first farm at Howbery near Wallingford about the year 1701, he succeeded in inventing the drill. He was experimenting with sainfoin, wishing to sow it by a new method, but his labourers objected. So he decided to construct a machine, and finally hit upon the principle of 'the groove, tongue, and spring in the soundboard of an organ', which suited his purpose admirably. In 1709 he removed to Prosperous Farm, Shalbourne, on the borders of Wiltshire and Berkshire, for the sake of his health and not, as his detractors subsequently said, owing to failure at Wallingford; and there he continued his experiments for over thirty years. It was at Prosperous, after a fruitful journey to France where he had observed intercultivation in the vineyards, that he evolved the horse hoe. Thus by using first the drill and then the horse hoe he was able to sow both corn and root crops at a controlled depth with a quarter of the customary seeding, and afterwards keep the ground free of weeds. As a result, he claimed to have grown as many as thirteen crops of wheat in succession on the same soil without manure. This, of course, was bad practice. In good farming, rotation and humus cannot be dispensed with, but Tull had done enough in providing the great agricultural Improvers who followed with two essential tools. The basic problem of rotation had already been solved by Weston.

The first among the large-scale Improvers was Charles, Viscount Townshend, who, on retiring from politics in middle age, devoted himself to the welfare of his estates at Raynham in Norfolk. He revived the use of marl as a dressing, was an enthusiast of Tull, adopted Weston's suggestions regarding turnips and grass, and evolved a crop sequence of his own, which eventually spread over most of the country under the title of the Norfolk four-course rotation. It consisted of Turnips, Barley, Seeds (Clover and Grass), and Wheat. Here was the anticipated revolution at last. 'Turnip' Townshend had both genius and good luck. Not only did he adopt and develop the discoveries of the past, but he was able, practically and on a large scale, to demonstrate their truth upon his own land. Nevertheless progress outside Norfolk was still slow. Forty years after

Townshend's death in 1738 another landowner in the same county took the lead. This was Thomas Coke, who inherited a family estate at Holkham at the age of twenty-two in 1776. At that date the rent roll brought in £2200 a year, but in 1816 it had risen to £20,000. Coke followed the principles of Weston, Tull, and Townshend and reclaimed many of his farms himself. In other cases he tactfully and enthusiastically educated his tenants, and guaranteed them the benefit of their improvements by offering long leases. He imported bone manure and cattle cake, and paid the greatest attention to breeding and to the cleaning and selection of grass seed. He held annual sheep shearings, originally meetings between himself and his friends to discuss farming problems, but which developed later into great gatherings of six hundred people or so, including distinguished guests from abroad. Coke's sheep shearings were, in fact, the forerunners of the agricultural shows. Other great landowners followed suit, e.g. the Duke of Bedford at Woburn, and Lord Leconfield at Petworth, and it was in large measure due to their work, particularly in crop husbandry, that England was able to modernize her agriculture so successfully during the emergency of the Napoleonic Wars. Improvement was not, however, the monopoly of the great. Mr T. Bedford Franklin, in his book *A History of Agriculture*,* quotes a yeoman ancestor, John Franklin, who in the late seventeenth and early eighteenth centuries was pioneering in the same way on his own small but *enclosed* farm. No doubt there were many others.

The eighteenth century also gave us the great pioneers in stock breeding, men of substance, whose work has been responsible for the establishment of British breeds all over the world. Until recently, their names were not often recorded

* Published by Bell.

in the standard history books, but they have brought as much honour and usually a great deal more wealth to this country than the general run of heroes. Robert Bakewell of Leicestershire produced a type of Longhorn suitable for beef, and a breed of Leicester sheep outstanding for mutton. This was most important, for the English wool trade had been declining for over a century. The new breeding sacrificed wool for mutton, but thereby restored the market for sheep. Bakewell also bred a successful type of black cart-horse, a native of Holland. Other livestock improvers included Robert Fowler; the Culleys; the Colling brothers, who established the Shorthorn, from which sprang the Lincoln Red (separately developed by Thomas Turnell); and John Ellman of Glynde, who improved Southdown sheep. In turn, most of the breeds of cattle, sheep, and pigs were taken up, the undesirable characteristics bred out, and the type fixed. By the second half of the eighteenth century the possibilities of improved farming and breeding had been clearly demonstrated, but the practice was still confined to a comparatively small proportion of the countryside; and until the demand for food seriously increased, agricultural progress was bound to be slow. However, the situation was already changing.

Shortly before 1700 Gregory King, an early statistician, had reckoned the population of the country at $5\frac{1}{2}$ millions, a figure we must accept for lack of better authority. It is fairly certain that by 1750 this total had not materially increased, but in 1801 the first official census gave the population of England and Wales as 9 millions, and thereafter it rose at a great rate. The ten-yearly statistics over the next half-century are as follows:

1811	10,164,256	1841	15,914,148
1821	12,000,236	1851	17,927,609
1831	13,896,797		

What were the cause and the effect of this increase?

No single answer can, of course, be given, but the principal cause, stated in general terms, was the Industrial Revolution, itself the expression of three impulses: the application of power to production (first water, then steam); the invention of machinery, mostly in the cotton, wool, and iron trades, and in coal mining; and the opportunism of comparatively few enterprising and energetic men with capital. The Industrial Revolution created opportunity and wealth which, however nebulous they seemed to him, yet did offer the ordinary man a prospect of prosperity and a variety of new jobs. By severing the bonds of technical production it abolished those restraints of common life which had hitherto kept the working man in his place. In the countryside it caused the repeal of the Act of Settlement which had crowded every parish with paupers for two hundred years, and it drew many of the rural unemployed into the factories and towns. There, it is true, conditions were bad enough, but at least they were due wholly to economic and not social forces, and, unlike the squirearchy, industrialism was not a rigid system incapable of change.

Besides this there were other factors that promoted the rise in population. Diet generally improved, owing to a gradual increase in the supply of fresh meat all the year round, the firstfruits of the Norfolk four-course rotation. Vaccination and a broad advance in medical science had a striking effect upon the death-rate; particularly upon infant mortality, which began at last to decline from the point where three-quarters of the children born in London died before the age of ten.

In general, therefore, two things,* opportunity (not security) and health, account briefly for this change, which in turn transformed agriculture and the village. The rising

* See also *A Land*, by Jacquetta Hawkes (Cresset Press), page 210.

population increased the demand for food, a demand which of its own volition would eventually have altered the economy of the countryside. In fact the wars with France between 1793 and 1815 made any gradual evolution impossible, for, once Napoleon had secured absolute power, virtually all imports from the Continent were cut off and home agriculture (as in subsequent twentieth-century wars) was forced to fill the gap. The old order of village farming was essentially a system of subsistence, inherited from an age that set hierarchy above efficiency. Its inadequacy in the face of the food shortages of the early 1800s, therefore, can easily be understood. To meet the needs of the new situation, agriculture had to undergo a drastic change – that was indisputable, else the country would have starved. All that had been done tentatively in the past by pioneers was now carried out wholesale on a national scale. Enclosure was the first step. Between 1760 and 1793, 1355 Enclosure Acts had been passed, but this number increased to 1934 between 1793 and 1815, a total of $5\frac{1}{2}$ million acres of land being enclosed in the whole of George III's reign, 1760–1820. In this latter period there were two distinct stages. First the open fields were taken in with a view to improving the output of existing cultivation. Then the commons and wastes were appropriated in order to bring new land into production, a more drastic step with greater social repercussions. This can readily be understood from the manner in which a private Enclosure Act was obtained.

In the first place the leading landowners and farmers in a parish met together and decided to enclose. Probably they settled their differences beforehand and made all necessary arrangements in private. In early days no public statement of their intention was required, but after 1774 notice of a scheme had to be posted on the church door for three Sundays during August or September. Next, they applied to

Parliament for permission to enclose, and a Bill was brought in, to which objections might be heard in committee. Unless there was serious opposition by a big owner, little notice was taken of complaints, certainly not of the petitions sent in by the small farmers and peasants, assuming the latter had been able to present their case in a proper manner at all. Three-quarters of those interested had to give their consent before the Bill could be passed, but since this proportion was calculated by property value, not numerically, there was rarely any difficulty. The Act then nominated three Commissioners (often neighbouring gentry) to investigate the claims and allocate the land, and also to decide such matters as liability for fencing and access to the new farms. In many cases land was given to the lord of the manor and to the titheholder; possibly a piece of ground was allotted to the poor. Otherwise every holder of land, provided his title was satisfactory, received his share. For many, the problem was to establish the validity of their title. Copyholders particularly suffered, owing to the disappearance of the Manor Rolls; likewise the great majority who enjoyed customary and common rights, of which there was no written record. Such rights stood little chance with the Commissioners. In other cases the properties allotted were too distant or inconvenient or unproductive to be of value to a villager, who could pay neither the fencing nor the legal costs incurred. Indeed the costs of enclosure were prohibitive: Mr Bedford Franklin quotes £1600 for Cosgrove in Northamptonshire, or about £1 per acre, of which one-third each was taken by law costs, roads and fences, and survey together with the fees of the Commissioners. In such a case a poor man had no alternative but to sell out to his more prosperous neighbour, and this happened in by far the majority of parishes. For many smallholders, and for most cottagers and squatters loss of land meant loss of independence, and there quickly arose a large class of labourers utterly dependent upon their wages for a living. Since the highest average rate never exceeded one shilling and sixpence a day, it was not possible to make ends meet on anything but a starvation scale. In the past, earnings had always been supplemented by milk and butter from a cow that grazed the commons, by a couple of pigs and some chickens that foraged for themselves in the woods, and by the produce of a strip. All that had now gone. In comparative terms, the rich became richer, the poor poorer, and the countryside was soon to be peopled by two main classes, the employers and the employed.

Looking back in history, it is hard to see how the technical changes that overtook agriculture could have been otherwise. Change was the direct result of economic pressure and, on balance, the advantages gained were very great. Farming became an industry and, once the land had been re-allotted and fenced, great progress was made all round. Production was quickly expanded by the introduction of primitive machinery and fertilizers, by the improvement of crops and stock, and by the general diffusion of technical knowledge. Roads, canals, and, later, railways enabled food to be easily distributed over the whole country, while profitable returns, especially from the sale of corn, attracted the investment of large quantities of capital in the industry. The result was that England was delivered from the effects of the Napoleonic blockade, and the countryside resolved itself into a pattern of fields, hedges, and farms much as we know it now.

On the other hand, the social misery that ensued might well have been avoided. Up to 1815 the profits yielded by the new farming were sufficient to benefit all classes, even assuming a higher cost of living and the loss of common land. If proper wages had been paid to the labourers the problem of poverty would have been partly solved. It is not true that the enclosed farms reduced work. In the long run they increased it, for the intensive cultivation of former open fields and commons required more labour than ever. Enclosure, however, threw a lot of labour on the market at once, and the farmers took advantage of this to keep wages down. In every parish there were unemployed, and when prices fell in 1814 just before the end of the French wars, their number increased. With no means of support, a man soon fell into pauperism and had to be kept on the rates. The administration of the Poor Law by the parish is described in detail in Part Two, but suffice it here to say that in order to reduce unemployment and the rates the parish officers hired out pauper labour on advantageous terms. This principle was taken a stage further by the Speenhamland system, which supplemented wages from the rates by a sliding scale of allowances, based on the price of bread and on the size of a man's family. The effects were disastrous. The farmers now had no call whatever to pay proper wages, knowing that the balance would be met by public assistance. The labourers found that bankruptcy paid almost as well as solvency, work or no work, and that a large family was a paying concern. Demoralization was therefore inevitable. Poverty was intensified, illegitimacy and the birth-rate increased, thrift, industry, and decency were discouraged. In many parishes more than 50 per cent of the working men were in receipt of poor relief, and rates exceeded 20s. in the pound.

The works of two contemporary writers are vividly descriptive of the condition of the age. Arthur Young (1741–1820) was an unsuccessful farmer turned journalist, publisher, and traveller. As the first Secretary to the Board of Agriculture, founded in 1793, he instituted a nation-wide inquiry into the state of agriculture, county by county.

Several of the reports he wrote or revised himself, and they remain today a most valuable source of information to the historian. Young saw both sides of the question. He was a keen advocate of enclosure on economic grounds, and maintained that only large-scale farming could take advantage of it. On the other hand, he was shocked by the social changes and he urged that sufficient land should always be set aside to enable every man to keep a cow and a garden. Of the misery around him he wrote as follows:

Go to an ale house kitchen of an old inclosed country, and there you will see the origin of poverty and the poor rates. For whom are they to be sober? For whom are they to save? For the parish? If I am diligent, shall I have leave to build a cottage? If I am sober, shall I have land for a cow? If I am frugal, shall I have half an acre for potatoes? You offer no motives; you have nothing but a parish officer and the workhouse. Bring me another pot.

In another passage his labourer says:

Parliament may be tender of property; all I know is that I had a cow and an Act of Parliament has taken it from me.

William Cobbett (1762–1835) also described the events of the times but with a political and partisan pen. As the son of a smallholder who lived near Farnham in Surrey, he began life working on the land but later sought his fortune in the army. After eight years' service he was discharged and took up journalism, first in America and then in England. Although of humble birth and continually at loggerheads with the authorities, Cobbett was no revolutionary. On the contrary he was a true Tory, deplored the commercialization of agriculture and resented the intrusion into the countryside of 'nouveaux riches', who took up farming for the purposes of prestige or profit. Like Young he was none too successful in his agricultural ventures, but that did not lessen the force of his strictures. He was aghast at the condition of the dispossessed peasants and labourers, and derided the ploughing and fencing of the commons, particularly where land was poor. He too toured the countryside and published his impressions in *Rural Rides*. Of Highclere in Hampshire he wrote:

We passed through the parish of *Highclere,* where they have *enclosed commons,* worth, as tillage land, not one single farthing an acre, and never will and never can be. As a common it afforded a little picking for geese and asses, and, in the moory parts of it, a little fuel for the labourers. But now it really can afford nothing. It will all fall to common again by degrees.

Cobbett had many prejudices, many of them stupid (such as his hatred of paper money), and he picked far too many quarrels, but he stood for the comparative humanity of the old order of the countryside that flourished before the Great Enclosures, and he never ceased to fight progress where it had been gained at the expense of the community.

The condition of country life described by Cobbett was representative of the whole period between the battle of Waterloo and the accession of Queen Victoria; the grimmest, perhaps, in the whole history of the village. This was true from every point of view. Not only was there an upheaval in the practice of farming and in the relations between the classes, but also the Industrial Revolution had undermined the only other source of income available to the countryman. Factory manufacture was steadily displacing handicrafts, and in each county noted for hand-made goods, and everywhere that rural craftsmen used to flourish, there was deepening depression and unemployment. As for the trades serving agriculture, these declined more slowly, for their direct connexion with the land could not immediately be severed by the mass-production methods of the town. The smith, the saddler, the thatcher, the wheel-wright, the carpenter, the mason, and to a less extent the woodman, the hedger, the basket-maker, and the hurdlemaker, were among the few independent craftsmen that survived the century in any force.

England defeated Napoleon, but the fruits of victory were very bitter. During the twenty years preceding Waterloo the cost of living had doubled, while the expenditure on poor relief had risen from less than £2 million in 1785 to nearly £8 million in 1817. At the height of the boom land had reached record prices; some farms sold for as much as fifty years' purchase, and farmers of every type had heavily mortgaged their property and stock to raise the ready cash. Prices began falling in 1813, but the end of the war two years later hastened their decline and ensured a slump. Arable farming suffered first and wheat prices dropped from 126s. a quarter in 1812 to 44s. in 1822. Pasture soon followed, with a similar fall in the value of livestock. Besides this, national expenditure which had stood at £20 million in 1792 rose to £106 million in 1815, and thereafter continued to rise. Thus taxation continued at a high level and added to the burdens of the community. Bankruptcies, forced sales, and orders to quit were the order of the day in the countryside, and either rents had to be substantially reduced or land abandoned, as indeed it was in many places. Moreover, rural unemployment was aggravated by the demobilization of soldiers and sailors; and the misery of persistent poverty brought many to desperation, for starvation respects no laws. Tension was increased by the behaviour of the authorities, who, now frightened, repressed all misdemeanours from petty theft to serious crime with extreme brutality and force. Poaching, the only alternative for countrymen with hungry families, was not the mild adventure it is now. Rather, it developed into relentless uncompromising warfare waged between enemies who knew that capture brought death or transportation to the offender.

Eventually there was serious disorder. The riots of 1830 and 1831 were the culmination of the long-drawn-out misery of the previous thirty years. They began in the summer of 1830 in Kent and soon spread to Sussex, Hampshire, Berkshire, and Wiltshire; the next year Dorset, Gloucestershire, and East Anglia were involved. In the south the outbreaks seem to have been organized; elsewhere action was disunited and sporadic. Destruction took the form of machinery-breaking as a protest against loss of work through mechanization, and of arson, particularly rickfiring, as an effective act of vengeance against employers. A rise in wages to two shillings or half-a-crown a day was generally demanded, and in some districts there was a good deal of sympathy for the men. The Government, however, took quite a different view, and Lord Melbourne, the Home Secretary, sent troops to quell the disorders and Special Commissioners to try the offenders. Sentences were indiscriminate and heavy. Although only one man lost his life in the riots, and he a rioter, 450 men and boys were transported to Australia, nine executed, and scores of others imprisoned. The famous example of the six labourers of Tolpuddle in Dorset, who tried to form a union as a more effective means of securing a living wage, was not exceptional; rather, it was representative of similar unrecorded cases. But the injustice of the Tolpuddle trial aroused public opinion at last, secured a free pardon for the men, and eventually brought them home again. Parliament, too, began a series of reforms which recognized the changed condition of the countryside and laid the foundations of recovery. But the peasant had lost his rights and his land, and the medieval economy of the countryside had finally passed away.

6

High Farming

By the accession of Queen Victoria the worst stages of transition were over. Several new Acts of Parliament had been passed which dealt actively with outstanding problems. The Reform Bill of 1832 redistributed the franchise, and awarded restricted representation in Parliament to the middle classes in the industrial and county towns, and to the farmers in the countryside. The Poor Law of 1834 put a general end to out-relief and reintroduced the workhouse as a test for the receipt of public assistance. The effects of this were far-reaching. The cost to the Exchequer was reduced by a half within seven years, and the parish was relieved of its heaviest burden. However, since Poor Law administration had been its principal duty for over two hundred years, the removal of this obligation resulted in the decline of the vestry as an effective instrument of village government. Also, since he could no longer rely on parish subsidies, the farmer was now compelled to pay a higher wage. Nevertheless wages rose very little: in 1837 the average weekly payment was less than 10s. 6d., an increase of only 8d. since 1824. The farmworker, although no longer a pauper, had still barely enough food to enable him to work, and his condition showed small improvement on the worst days of Enclosure twenty years before. Even now the open fields and commons had not quite disappeared, and it required two more Acts, passed in 1836 and in 1845, to remove them. A few managed to escape altogether – in the parish of Laxton in Nottinghamshire, for example, and a number of commons and village greens that have fortunately been preserved as public playing fields and open spaces. Yet another important piece of legislation was the Tithe Commutation Act of 1836 that abolished tithing in kind and substituted a money rent based on the average price of corn over seven years. Later in the century the owner was compelled to bear this charge, not the occupier of the land, but already the whole relationship of landlord and tenant was undergoing a change. The tremendous fluctuations experienced by the tenant since 1800 had made him chary of doing improvements. Much of the land brought into cultivation during the boom years had now reverted, and the landlord was being forced to accept liability for some part of the farm's equipment and upkeep, although no law had yet been passed by which the financial burdens of farming were properly shared, and the tenant given reasonable security of tenure.

By this time, also, the number of yeomen had seriously dwindled, for the reasons outlined in the previous chapter. There is no better description of a yeoman in decline than Richard Jefferies' portrait of his father in *Amaryllis at the Fair*. Although written in 1887 the moral and veracity of the book apply equally to an earlier age. James Luckett Jefferies was a fine character and, by all accounts, a hard-working man. His standards were high, too high probably for the times, for everything that was done had to be done perfectly — from the making and setting of a gate to the planting of a patch of potatoes. He was a large eater, a healthy, solid man, and no fool. But with all this he had a strong streak of pessimism, induced, one gathers, by his inability to make the farm* pay. The problem was largely economic. Forty acres had been a good holding before the Enclosures. It was not adequate now. Such was the fate of many others of Jefferies' kind in the early nineteenth century.

* Coate Farm, near Swindon, Wiltshire.

The period between 1832 and 1853 was one of preparation, for agriculture took longer than manufacturing industry to recover its equilibrium. Parliamentary action has already been described, but much was done by agriculturists themselves. In 1840 the Royal Agricultural Society of England, with Queen Victoria as its patron, received its Charter. It was a symptom of initiative, for it immediately attracted a number of the best brains and most enterprising landowners and farmers, now no longer represented by a few exceptional men as in the late eighteenth century. Since that date, now more than a century ago, the Society has continually fostered invention and research and has provided a national Show of world-wide reputation that has stimulated progress in every branch of farming. There soon followed other important foundations – for example, the Agricultural College at Cirencester, and the Experimental Station at Rothamsted with which are associated the names of Sir John Lawes and Sir Henry Gilbert. These two men scientifically investigated the value of manures, in part basing their work upon the discoveries of Justus Liebig, the German chemist; they also studied crop rotations and the properties of cattle foods. Similar progress was made in geology, ecology, botany, in all branches of animal study, and in engineering as applied to the land. Steam was now being introduced as a motive power for ploughing and threshing, and new or improved implements and labour-saving machinery, such as cultivators, rollers, drills, reapers, mowing machines, horse-rakes, elevators, turnip and chaff cutters, and many others all began making an appearance. Porous clay pipes, invented by John Reade in 1843, solved many of the problems of field drainage, which was widely practised after the middle of the century.

Technically there was ample evidence of renewed progress in the whole field of English agriculture. Economically the outlook was a little less optimistic, but farm prices were gradually improving in response to the demands of the towns and the growing population. By taxing foreign corn the Corn Laws continued to protect the arable farmers, and in 1839 wheat stood as high as 70s. a quarter. However, pressure from the manufacturers was growing, and the Anti-Corn-Law League led by Cobden soon had a large middle-class following in the towns. In agitating for repeal, the townsmen argued that the free import of foreign corn would provide cheap food for the working classes, would encourage the sale of British manufactured goods abroad, and would discourage the setting-up of foreign industry. The landed interests naturally thought otherwise. They denied that the working classes would automatically benefit from cheap food; rather, they said, it would enable employers to reduce wages. Agriculture would be ruined and farm labourers would lose their employment. Free Trade, however, was on the way, and the Irish potato famine of 1845, necessitating urgent supplies of corn to prevent starvation, forced the hand of the Conservative Prime Minister, Sir Robert Peel. The Corn Laws were repealed and import duty was reduced in stages to 1s. a quarter by 1849. Later it was abolished altogether. At this juncture Disraeli, who had opposed Peel, his own party leader, made an historic speech in which he foretold the ruin of the land, and at the time his fears seemed amply justified. Between 1848 and 1852 prices did fall, and there was a mild panic when wheat dropped to 38s. a quarter. The real depression, however, was not yet. For various reasons it was delayed for over twenty years, by which time Disraeli had forgotten his dark words. In the interim, from 1853 to 1874, British agriculture, especially in the south, enjoyed an era of prosperity and progress known to historians and others as the 'golden age' or 'high farming' or merely the 'good old days'! It was due, in part, to a succession of lucky circumstances, whereby (once the Crimean War was over) England was at peace, and free to develop her own industries, while much of the rest of the world was disturbed. Russian trade was suffering from the consequences of the Crimea; America, still undeveloped, was torn by the Civil War of 1861–5; Germany was involved in a series of campaigns – with Denmark in 1853, with Austria in 1866, and with France in 1870–1. Each of these events stimulated British exports and diverted the import of foreign food, with the result that home agriculture experienced little competition and prospered exceedingly.

It was a wonderful age. Inventions and improvements came into their own, livestock breeding flourished, and the general level of farming rose quickly. Seasons were favourable, prices high in all branches of farm production, and money was poured into the land. All over the country, in a variety of styles and materials, new farmhouses and steadings were being put up, and old ones rebuilt, and all exhibited a monumental solidity. In many cases the workmanship was so good that a century has made little difference to their condition. Yet it is this very quality, this ability to endure, that has depreciated their value to-day. Many of the barns and shippons are difficult to alter, and changing methods demand adaptability in buildings as well as in farm practice. As memorials of wealth, however, they remain at all times impressive.

Parallel with farm building, many landowners added new cottages to their estates. Sometimes whole villages were remodelled. Alfred Williams, the Wiltshire poet, describes one in his book *Villages of the White Horse.** In spite of being written sixty years later, and notwithstanding the naïveté which is characteristic of the author, the

* Published by Duckworth.

description is interesting and generally true. (See Plate 6 (a)).

A little more than a mile east of Earl's Court [near Swindon], perched upon a small hill, and surrounded with tall elms, beeches, and apple orchards, the rosy-white bloom of which scents the air with fragrance in the early summer, is the pretty village of Bourton, whose inhabitants, undisturbed by the noises and fever of whirling life, dwell in peace and quiet, and follow their pursuits on the farm, leading a simple, guileless existence. Here every house and building is of stone, well made, with large gardens, and plenty of room and light; it is altogether a model village. This was brought about by a beneficent landlord, who came a stranger, and sympathized with the poor; he had all the ruinous cottages removed and filled their places with substantial modern dwellings. Nearly every cottage has gardens and parterre in front; these the occupants tend with great pride and care, vying with each other in the production of beautiful blooms.

The stranger to whom Williams refers was a wealthy town merchant turned squire – a common Victorian phenomenon; he also provided a church and a school. Similarly Alfred Williams' own village nearby, South Marston, was supplied with model cottages and a school in the late 1860s; his father and grandfather were employed there as the principal carpenters. These are but two examples of large-scale social improvements. Gardens were certainly a great boon, but a number of landowners offered allotments as well. These were not new, for, as the name implies, they had first appeared at the time of the Great Enclosures as compensation for the loss of holdings in the open fields. Parish farms had also been tried, but without success. Allotments, however, caught on and were officially encouraged, although their provision had never been made obligatory under Act of Parliament. Some farmers opposed them on the grounds that it made the labourer too independent; that he might reserve his best efforts for his own ground, or steal the farmer's corn for feeding stock, or that there was no land to spare. Nevertheless allotments steadily increased; no less than 914 existed on the Duke of Marlborough's estates, and nearly 400 on Lord Shaftesbury's. Their value has been variously estimated, for they could only be had under stringent conditions of good behaviour, but a quarter-acre plot is said to have added about two to four shillings to the weekly wage. At first, grain was grown, but when the price fell after 1874 the labourer turned to vegetables and fruit for the house, and kept a pig if he could.

From all this it might be concluded that the agricultural labourer was at last receiving his just reward. In fact, although rents and profits rose sharply between 1853 and 1862, wages still lagged a long way behind. In 1860 the average nominal rate was a little over 11s. 6d. a week, in 1870 12s. 2d., very little more than in the depression days of the 1830s. In winter and at slack times a man earned less, and this meant that he usually had to depend upon the labour of his wife and children in order to make ends meet. Often his family, if a large one, earned more than he did, and this had two evil effects. It kept wages down and it encouraged child and female labour. In the Eastern Counties there developed a system known as Gang Labour, which consisted of the employment by farmers of troops of men, women, and children, who had no home, but wandered about doing field work under the direction of gang-masters. They slept in barns and ate what they could and earned practically nothing. Public opinion was finally aroused, and the practice was controlled first by the Gangs Act of 1868 and then by various Education Acts after 1870, by which all children up to the age of fourteen were sent to school, none to be employed on the land, except by permission at busy periods of the year. Even then the rule was frequently broken, as school attendance registers show.

For a faithful portrait of English labouring life in mid-Victorian times, it is still best to turn to the letter written to *The Times* in November 1872 by Richard Jefferies, then an unknown Swindon reporter. Although written from the standpoint of the tenant farmer, and tinged here and there with condescension, it remains a classical example of social reporting. It is printed here in full.

SIR,

The Wiltshire agricultural labourer is not so highly paid as those of Northumberland, nor so low as those of Dorset; but in the amount of his wages, as in intelligence and general position, he may fairly be taken as an average specimen of his class throughout a large portion of the kingdom.

As a man, he is usually strongly built, broad-shouldered, and massive in frame, but his appearance is spoilt by the clumsiness of his walk and the want of grace in his movements. Though quite as large in muscle, it is very doubtful if he possesses the strength of the seamen who may be seen lounging about the ports. There is a want of firmness, a certain disjointed style, about his limbs, and the muscles themselves have not the hardness and tension of the sailor's. The labourer's muscle is that of a cart-horse, his motions lumbering and slow. His style of walk is caused by following the plough in early childhood, when the weak limbs find it a hard labour to pull the heavy-nailed boots from the thick clay soil. Ever afterwards he walks as if it were an exertion to lift his legs. His food may, perhaps, have something to do with the deadened slowness which seems to pervade everything he does – there seems a lack of vitality about him. It consists chiefly of bread and cheese, with bacon twice or thrice a week, varied with onions, and if he be a milker (on some farms) with a good 'tuck-out' at his employer's expense on Sundays. On ordinary days he dines at the fashionable hour of six or seven in the evening – that is, about that time his cottage scents the road with a powerful odour of boiled cabbage, of which he eats an immense quantity. Vegetables are his luxuries, and a large garden, therefore, is the greatest blessing he can have. He eats huge onions raw; he has no idea of flavouring his food with them, nor of making those savoury and inviting messes or vegetable soups at which the French peasantry are so clever. In Picardy I have often dined in a peasant's cottage, and thoroughly enjoyed the excellent soup he puts upon the table for his ordinary meal. To dine in an English labourer's cottage would be impossible. His bread is generally good, certainly; but his bacon is the cheapest he can buy at small second-class shops – oily, soft, wretched stuff; his vegetables are cooked in detestable style, and eaten saturated with the pot-liquor. Pot-liquor is a favourite soup. I have known cottagers actually apply at farmers' kitchens, not only for the pot-liquor in which meat has been soddened, but for the water in which potatoes have been boiled – potato-liquor – and sup it up with avidity. And this not in times of dearth or scarcity, but rather as a relish. They never buy anything but bacon; never butcher's meat. Philanthropic ladies, to my knowledge, have demonstrated over and over again even to their limited capacities that certain parts of butchers' meat can be bought just as cheap, and will make more savoury and nutritive food; and even now, with the present high price of meat, a certain portion would be advantageous. In vain; the labourers obstinately adhere to the pig, and the pig only. When, however, an opportunity does occur, the amount of food they will eat is something astonishing. Once a year, at the village club dinner, they gormandize to repletion. In one instance I knew of a man eating a plate of roast beef (and the slices are cut enormously thick at these dinners), a plate of boiled beef, then another of boiled mutton, and then a fourth of roast mutton, and a fifth of ham. He said he could not do much to the bread and cheese; but didn't he go into the pudding! I have even heard of men stuffing to the fullest extent of their powers, and then retiring from the table to take an emetic of mustard and return to a second gorging. There is scarcely any limit to their power of absorbing beer. I have known reapers and mowers make it their boast that they could lie on their backs and never take the wooden bottle (in the shape of a small barrel) from their lips till they had drunk a gallon, and from the feats I have seen I verily believe it a fact. The beer they get is usually poor and thin, though sometimes in harvest the farmers bring out a taste of strong liquor, but not till the work is nearly over; for from this very practice of drinking enormous quantities of small beer the labourer cannot drink more than a very limited amount of good liquor without getting tipsy. This is why he so speedily gets inebriated at the alehouse. While mowing and reaping many of them lay in a small cask.

They are much better clothed now than formerly. Corduroy trousers and slops are the usual style. Smock-frocks are going out of use, except for milkers and faggers. Almost every labourer has his Sunday suit, very often really good clothes, sometimes glossy black, with the regulation 'chimney-pot'. His unfortunate walk betrays him, dress how he will. Since labour has become so expensive it has become a common remark among the farmers that the labourer will go to church in broadcloth and the masters in smock-frocks. The labourer never wears gloves – that has to come with the march of the times; but he is particularly choice over his necktie. The women must dress in the fashion. A very respectable draper in an agricultural district was complaining to me the other day that the poorest class of women would have everything in the fashionable style, let it change as often as it would. In former times, if he laid in a stock of goods suited to tradesmen, and farmers' wives and daughters, if the fashion changed, or they got out of date, he could dispose of them easily to the servants. Now no such thing. The quality did not matter so much, but the style must be the style of the day – no sale for remnants. The poorest girl, who had not got two yards of flannel on her back, must have the same style of dress as the squire's daughter – Dolly Vardens, chignons, and parasols for ladies who can work all day reaping in the broiling sun of August! Gloves, kid, for hands that milk the cows!

The cottages now are infinitely better than they were. There is scarcely room for further improvement in the cottages now erected upon estates. They have three bedrooms, and every appliance and comfort compatible with their necessarily small size. It is only the cottages erected by the labourers themselves on

waste plots of ground which are open to objection. Those he
builds himself are indeed, as a rule, miserable huts, disgraceful to
a Christian country. I have an instance before me at this moment
where a man built a cottage with two rooms and no staircase or
upper apartments, and in those two rooms eight persons lived and
slept – himself and wife, grown-up daughters, and children.
There was not a scrap of garden attached, not enough to grow
half a dozen onions. The refuse and sewage was flung into the
road, or filtered down a ditch into the brook which supplied that
part of the village with water. In another case at one time there
was a cottage in which twelve persons lived. This had upper
apartments, but so low was the ceiling that a tall man could stand
on the floor, with his head right through the opening for the staircase, and see along the upper floor under the beds! These squatters are the curse of the community. It is among them that fever
and kindred infectious diseases break out; it is among them that
wretched couples are seen bent double with rheumatism and
affections of the joints caused by damp. They have often been
known to remain so long, generation after generation, in these
wretched hovels that at last the lord of the manor having neglected
to claim quit-rent, they can defy him, and claim them as their own
property, and there they stick, eyesores and blots, the fungi of the
land. The cottages erected by farmers or by landlords are now,
one and all, fit and proper habitations for human beings; and I
verily believe it would be impossible throughout the length and
breadth of Wiltshire to find a single bad cottage on any large
estate, so well and so thoroughly have the landed proprietors done
their work. On all farms gardens are attached to the cottages, in
many instances very large, and always sufficient to produce enough
vegetables for the resident. In villages the allotment system has
been greatly extended of late years, and has been found most
beneficial, both to owners and tenants. As a rule the allotments are
let at a rate which may be taken as £4 per annum – a sum which
pays the landlord very well, and enables the labourer to re-
munerate himself. In one village which came under my observation the clergyman of the parish has turned a portion of his
glebe-land into allotments – a most excellent and noble example,

which cannot be too widely followed or too much extolled. He is thus enabled to benefit almost every one of his poor parishioners, and yet without destroying that sense of independence which is the great characteristic of a true Englishman. He has issued a book of rules and conditions under which these allotments are held, and he thus places a strong check upon drunkenness and dissolute habits, indulgence in which is a sure way to lose the portions of ground. There is scarcely an end to the benefits of the allotment system. In villages there cannot be extensive gardens, and the allotments supply their place. The extra produce above that which supplies the table and pays the rent is easily disposed of in the next town, and places many additional comforts in the labourer's reach. The refuse goes to help support and fatten the labourer's pig, which brings him in profit enough to pay the rent of his cottage, and the pig, in turn, manures the allotment. Some towns have large common lands, held under certain conditions; such are Malmesbury, with 500 acres, and Tetbury (the common land of which extends two miles): both these being arable, etc. These are not exactly in the use of labourers, but they are in the hands of a class to which the labourer often rises. Many labourers have fruit trees in their gardens which, in some seasons, prove very profitable. In the present year, to my knowledge, a labourer sold £4 worth of apples; and another made £3 10s. of the produce of one pear-tree, pears being scarce.

To come at last to the difficult question of wages. In Wiltshire there has been no extended strike, and very few meetings upon the subject, for the simple reason that the agitators can gain no hold upon a county where, as a mass, the labourers are well paid. The common day-labourer receives 10s., 11s., and 12s. a week, according to the state of supply and demand for labour in various districts, and, if he milks, 1s. more, making 13s. a week, now common wages. These figures are rather below the mark; I could give instances of much higher pay. To give a good idea of the wages paid, I will take the case of a hill farmer (arable, Marlborough Downs), who paid this last summer during harvest 18s. per week per man. His reapers often earned 10s. a day; enough to pay their year's rent in a week. These men lived in cottages on the farm, with three bedrooms each, and some larger, with every modern appliance, each having a garden of a quarter of an acre attached and close at hand, for which cottage and garden they paid 1s. per week rent. The whole of these cottages were insured by the farmer himself, their furniture, etc., in one lump, and the insurance policy cost him, as nearly as possible, 1s. 3d. per cottage per year. For this he deducted 1s. per year each from their wages. None of the men would have insured unless he had insisted upon doing it for them. These men had from six to eight quarts of beer per man (over and above their 18s. per week) during harvest every day. In spring and autumn their wages are much increased by forced work, hoeing, etc. In winter the farmer draws their coal for them in his waggons, a distance of eight miles from the nearest wharf, enabling them to get it at cost price. This is no slight advantage, for, at the present high price of coal, it is sold, delivered in the villages, at 2s. per cwt. Many who cannot afford it in the week buy a quarter of a cwt. on Saturday night to cook their Sunday's dinner with, for 6d. This is at the rate of £2 per ton. Another gentleman, a large steam cultivator in the Vale, whose name is often before the public, informs me that his books show that he paid £100 in one year in cash to one cottage for labour, showing the advantage the labourer possesses over the mechanic, since his wife and child can add to his income. Many farmers pay £50 and £60 a year for beer drunk by their labourers – a serious addition to their wages. The railway companies and others who employ mechanics do not allow them any beer. The allowance of a good cottage and a quarter of an acre of garden for 1s. per week is not singular. Many who were at the Autumn Manoeuvres of the present year may remember having a handsome row of houses, rather than cottages, pointed out to them as inhabited by labourers at 1s. per week. In the immediate neighbourhood of large manufacturing towns 1s. 6d. a week is sometimes paid; but then these cottages would in such positions readily let to mechanics for 3s., 4s., and even 5s. per week. There was a great outcry when the Duke of Marlborough issued an order that the cottages on his estate should in future only be let to such men as worked upon the farms where those cottages are situated. In reality this was the very greatest blessing the Duke could have conferred upon the agricultural labourer; for it insured him a good cottage at a nearly nominal rent and close to his work; whereas in many instances previously the cottages on the farms had been let at a high rate to the mechanics, and the labourer had to walk miles before he got to his labour. Cottages are not erected by landowners or by farmers as paying speculations. It is well known that the condition of things prevents the agricultural labourer from being able to pay a sufficient rent to be a fair percentage upon the sum expended. In one instance a landlord has built some cottages for his tenant, the tenant paying a certain amount of interest on the sum invested by the landlord. Now, although this is a matter of arrangement, and not of speculation – that is, although the interest paid by the tenant is a low percentage upon the money laid out, yet the rent paid by the labourers inhabiting these cottages to the tenant does not reimburse him what he pays his landlord as interest – not by a considerable margin. But then he has the advantage of his labourers close to his work, always ready at hand.

Over and above the actual cash wages of the labourer, which are now very good, must be reckoned his cottage and garden, and often a small orchard, at a nominal rent, his beer at his master's expense, piecework, gleaning after harvest, etc., which alter his real position very materially. In Gloucestershire, on the Cotswolds, the best-paid labourers are the shepherds, for in that great sheep country much trust is reposed in them. At the annual auction of shearlings which are held upon the low farms a purse is made for the shepherd of the flock, into which everyone who attends is expected to drop a shilling, often producing £5. The shepherds on the Wiltshire downs are also well paid, especially in lambing time, when the greatest watchfulness and care are required. It has been stated that the labourer has no chance of rising from his position. This is sheer cant. He has very good opportunities of rising, and often does rise, to my knowledge. At this present moment I could mention a person who has risen from a position scarcely equal to that of a labourer, not only to have a farm himself, but to place his sons in farms. Another has just entered on a farm; and several more are on the high-road to that desirable consummation. If a labourer possesses any amount of intelligence he becomes head carter or head fagger, as the case may be; and from that to be assistant or underbailiff, and finally bailiff. As a bailiff he has every opportunity to learn the working of a farm, and is often placed in entire charge of a farm at a distance from his employer's residence. In time he establishes a reputation as a practical man, and being in receipt of good wages, with very little expenditure, saves some money. He has now little difficulty in obtaining the promise of a farm, and with this can readily take up money. With average care he is a made man. Others rise from petty trading, petty dealing with pigs and calves, till they save sufficient to rent a small farm, and make that the basis of larger dealing operations. I question very much whether a clerk in a firm would not find it much more difficult, as requiring larger capital, to raise himself to a level with his employer than an agricultural labourer does to the level of a farmer.

Many labourers now wander far and wide as navvies, etc., and perhaps when these return home, as most of them do, to agricultural labour, they are the most useful and intelligent of their class, from a readiness they possess to turn their hand to anything. I know one at this moment who makes a large addition to his ordinary wages by brewing for the small inns, and very good liquor he brews, too. They pick up a large amount of practical knowledge.

The agricultural women are certainly not handsome; I know no peasantry so entirely uninviting. Occasionally there is a girl whose nut-brown complexion and sloe-black eyes are pretty, but their features are very rarely good, and they get plain quickly, so soon as the first flush of youth is past. Many have really good hair in abundance, glossy and rich, perhaps from its exposure to the fresh air. But on Sundays they plaster it with strong-smelling pomade and hair-oil, which scents the air for yards most unpleasantly. As a rule, it may safely be laid down that the agricultural women are moral, far more so than those of the town. Rough and rude jokes and language are, indeed, too common; but that is all. No evil comes of it. The fairs are the chief cause of immorality. Many an honest, hard-working servant-girl owes her ruin to these fatal mops and fairs, when liquor to which she is unaccustomed overcomes her. Yet it seems cruel to take from them the one day or two of the year on which they can enjoy themselves fairly in their own fashion. The spread of friendly societies, patronized by the gentry and clergy, with their annual festivities, is a remedy which is gradually supplying them with safer, and yet congenial, amusement. In what may be termed lesser morals I cannot accord either them or the men the same praise. They are too ungrateful for the many great benefits which are bountifully supplied them – the brandy, the soup, and fresh meat readily extended without stint from the farmer's home in sickness to the cottage are too quickly forgotten. They who were most benefited are often the first to most loudly complain and to backbite. Never once in all my observation have I heard a labouring man or woman make a grateful remark; and yet I can confidently say that there is no class of persons in England who receive so many attentions and benefits from their superiors as the agricultural labourers. Stories are rife of their even refusing to work at disastrous fires because beer was not immediately forthcoming. I trust this is not true; but it is too much in character. No term is too strong in condemnation, for those persons who endeavour to arouse an agitation among a class of people so shortsighted and so ready to turn against their own benefactors and their own interest. I am credibly informed that one of these agitators, immediately after the Bishop of Gloucester's unfortunate but harmlessly intended speech at the Gloucester Agricultural Society's dinner – one of these agitators mounted a platform at a village meeting and in plain language incited and advised the labourers to duck the farmers! The agricultural women either go out to field-work or become indoor servants. In harvest they hay-make – chiefly light work, as raking; and reap, which is much harder labour; but then, while reaping, they work their own time, as it is done by the piece. Significantly enough, they make longer hours while reaping. They are notoriously late to arrive, and eager to return home on the hay-field. The children help both in haymaking and reaping. In spring and autumn they hoe and do other piecework. On pasture farms they beat clots or pick up stones out of the way of the mowers' scythes. Occasionally, but rarely now, they milk. In winter they wear gaiters, which give the ankles a most ungainly appearance. Those who go out to service get very low wages at first from their extreme awkwardness, but generally quickly rise. As dairymaids they get very good wages indeed. Dairymaids are scarce and valuable. A dairymaid who can be trusted to take charge of a dairy will sometimes get £20 besides her board (liberal) and sundry perquisites. These often save money, marry bailiffs, and help their husbands to start a farm.

In the education provided for children Wiltshire compares favourably with other counties. Long before the passing of the recent Act in reference to education the clergy had established schools in almost every parish, and their exertions have enabled the greater number of places to come up to the standard required by the Act, without the assistance of a School Board. The great difficulty is the distance children have to walk to school, from the sparseness of the population and the number of outlying hamlets. This difficulty is felt equally by the farmers, who, in the majority of cases, find themselves situated far from a good school. In only one place has anything like a cry for education arisen, and that is on the extreme northern edge of the country. The Vice-Chairman of the Swindon Chamber of Agriculture recently stated that only one-half of the entire population of Inglesham could read and write. It subsequently appeared that the parish of Inglesham was very sparsely populated, and that a variety of circumstances had prevented vigorous efforts being made. The children, however, could attend schools in adjoining parishes, not farther than two miles, a distance which they frequently walk in other parts of the country.

Those who are so ready to cast every blame upon the farmer, and to represent him as eating up the earnings of his men and enriching himself with their ill-paid labour, should remember that farming, as a rule, is carried on with a large amount of borrowed capital. In these days, when £6 an acre has been expended in growing roots for sheep, when the slightest derangement of calculation in the price of wool, meat, or corn, or the loss of a crop, seriously interferes with a fair return for capital invested, the farmer has to sail extremely close to the wind, and only a little more would find his canvas shaking. It was only recently that the cashier of the principal bank of an agricultural county, after an unprosperous year, declared that such another season would make almost every farmer insolvent. Under these circumstances it is really to be wondered at that they have done as much as they have for the labourer in the last few years, finding him with better cottages, better wages, better education, and affording him better opportunities of rising in the social scale.

I am, Sir, faithfully yours,

RICHARD JEFFERIES

Coate Farm, Swindon
November 12

7

Rural Decline

In 1874 trade in Britain experienced a depression. During the previous decade exports had been stimulated by a series of events that were not likely to recur – intensive construction of railways in Europe and America, the opening of the Suez Canal, and the Franco-Prussian War. In due course these incentives to production receded, and the market was unable to absorb the new rate of output. It was a situation that affected not only Britain but also many other parts of the world. In the United States it had the effect of driving thousands out of the towns to settle new lands in the middle and far west, a movement of profound significance to British agriculture. In Britain itself, farming first felt the wind through a series of bad harvests. The summer of 1879 was catastrophic, the wettest season on record, but any rise in the price of grain was forestalled by a flood of cheap American corn, grown in a favourable climate upon the virgin soils of the newly broken prairies. Arable farming, hampered by lack of landspace, by uncertain weather, and by the disabilities of tradition, never recovered and the bottom fell out of corn production. The home market, increasingly open to foreign competition through the acceleration of transport and communications, was able less and less to absorb the produce of British farms. A slight respite in the 1880s due to rent remissions and the expenditure of reserves accumulated in the period of prosperity was followed by a further blow. Hitherto the prices of fat cattle, pigs, and sheep had remained firm, but with the advent of refrigeration even that market was lost. From 1890 onwards dead meat from America, Argentina, New Zealand, and Australia poured into the country. Cheese, butter, and wool were also heavily imported, and there were now no more reserves with which to face bad times. In addition agricultural recovery was increasingly hampered by the structure of the nation's trade. Industry in Britain had developed to such a degree that it now depended for its existence upon the export of vast quantities of manufactured goods. In the eyes of the manufacturers these could best be exchanged for raw materials and for cheap food; one fed the machines, the other fed the people, of whom already far the larger proportion lived in towns. In this way foreign food kept the export trade alive, and industry had an interest in the depression of home agriculture.

The consequences of this situation were duly reflected in the condition and appearance of the countryside. Between 1871 and 1901 the corn area of the country declined by nearly three million acres, and the stubbles fell back to some sort of grass. Buildings decayed, fences were neglected, roads were not repaired, and some farmsteads were completely abandoned – these were the tokens of the times. Worse still – for material things can generally be replaced – the people themselves began rapidly to leave the land. Agricultural labourers alone decreased by over 300,000 in thirty years; farmers also were less, although in their case the decline was not so steep and there were some notable survivals. The findings of various Commissions of Inquiry, and the evidence gathered by Sir H. Rider Haggard in his monumental survey of twenty-seven English counties* confirmed the absolute inferiority of the place now held by agriculture in the national economy.

Rider Haggard, in a lucid conclusion to his work, ascribes this tragedy to the influence of Free Trade, and to

* *Rural England*, Longmans, 1902.

the consequent decay of village life. He considered that the landlord had suffered most, and that landownership would survive only where it was bolstered up by other investments or where it was altogether a matter of luxury and prestige. He thought that only two kinds of farmers could make a living – the big man, actively using capital to convert land, plant, and stock to a type of farming based almost entirely on grass husbandry, and the small man who employed no labour but that of himself and his family. The middle-class farmer – the yeoman, in other words – had little hope. The labourer, on the other hand, was better off than formerly; his wages had risen (in 1898 they averaged over 14 shillings a week), but his housing was wretched and there was no call for him to remain in a depressed industry and in a dying village; the town offered far better prospects all round. Such were Rider Haggard's principal observations. The solutions he offered were no less discouraging, for he realized that the only radical cure was Protection, as in other countries; but in England – now a heavily industrialized and urbanized country wedded to Free Trade – this was impossible. The doctrine of cheap food was firmly implanted for ever in the minds of every class, even in the countryside. Instead he urged that more effective powers should be granted to the President of the Board of Agriculture to operate Credit Banks, co-operative marketing and State subsidies for rural housing. He also advocated better rural education and the introduction of an 'Agricultural Post', a special transport service to compete with the railways and carry agricultural goods at cheap rates. As to farm practice, it was clear that the only way to make a living was to sell liquid milk, develop market garden and fruit crops, and multiply pigs and poultry, fed on cheap imported grain.

Rider Haggard was particularly severe on Parliament, which had done nothing radical to save agriculture. A

Department of Agriculture had been established in 1889, a direct successor to the Board of Agriculture served by Arthur Young and abolished in 1822, but its scope was limited. Such legislation as came into force at the end of the century was designed to alleviate farming troubles, not prevent or cure them. These were technical measures controlling animal diseases and the purity of seeds and feeding stuffs; allowing tenant farmers compensation for improvements and greater security of tenure; encouraging small-holdings and allotments; lessening local taxation. Perhaps the most far-reaching measures affecting the countryside were the new social laws. For instance, the franchise was extended to agricultural labourers in 1884. The Education Acts of 1870, 1873, and 1876 and a whole range of supplementary Acts enforced the attendance of all children between the ages of five and fourteen either at denominational schools or at new State elementary schools. Administration was vested first in locally elected School Boards or Attendance Committees, but later transferred, by the Act of 1902, to the newly formed County Councils. This same Act permitted the foundation of State secondary schools to extend the work of independent grammar schools in educating the more advanced and older pupils. Local government was entirely recast by the Acts of 1888 and 1894; the former instituted County Councils, the latter Rural District Councils and Parish Councils. Hitherto the countryside had been governed by the Justices of the Peace and by the vestries, together with a bewildering variety of independent bodies charged with special duties – poor law, highways, sanitary questions, and so forth. Most of these duties were now transferred to the Local Government Authority, and the entire administration was simplified, extended, and improved.

Another source of change was the work of the agricultural

Unions. Between 1834 and 1872 there had been few attempts at organization among the agricultural labourers. However, as prosperity increased in the 1850s and 1860s and as associations of industrial workers were formed in the towns, so the spirit of combination returned to the country-side. Between 1871 and 1875 the Trades Union and various amending Acts were passed, legalizing the status of Unions and establishing their right to bargain on behalf of their members. This set the stage for further advance, and in February 1872 Joseph Arch was asked to found a local Trade Union of farm workers at Wellesbourne in War-wickshire. Arch was a Liberal and a Primitive Methodist preacher, and therefore a man of spirit and intelligence; be-sides this he was a skilled workman and a contractor for hedge-laying and fieldwork which brought him a certain economic security: thus he was dependent neither on wages nor on the whims of a master for his living. A thousand people attended his first public meeting, and at his second a committee was elected and a secretary appointed to organize a Union. Almost immediately a number of branches and village Unions sprang up within the district, and the move-ment, which was well publicized, encouraged similar activity up and down the country. Arch and his friends were in demand everywhere, and many prominent men, mostly Liberals, gave support.

On 29 May, at a conference of delegates from all the local Unions held at Leamington, it was decided to set up *The National Agricultural Labourers' Union* under the chairmanship of Arch. This was the first national Trade Union for farm workers. The entrance fee was 6d., the weekly contribution 2d. A year later the membership had risen to 71,835 and the number of branches to 982, spread over every English county except six. At first the objects of the Union were, in Arch's own words, 'to raise wages, shorten the hours, and make a man out of a land-tied slave'. But soon the scope was widened – the vote was demanded, likewise, the disestablishment of the Church, changes in legislation, and land for the labourers. In addition, the Union carried on the work of a Friendly Society, all of which tended to weaken its ability to achieve the primary objects of raising wages and shortening hours. The founding of the 'National' did not prevent the formation of other local Unions, of which there were several, e.g. *The Lincolnshire Labour League, The South Lancashire Protective Association, The West of England Union*; and these, while retaining their independence, set up a joint executive committee with the title of *The Federal Union of Labourers*, which corresponded in influence to the 'National'. An early result of all this activity was a small rise in wages in a variety of counties, but considerable resistance was offered by the farmers. Often a dispute was settled by the Unions sending their members elsewhere in the country or overseas. It was officially stated that between 1871 and 1881 over 700,000 men, women, and children emigrated in this way, but it caused a heavy drain on Union funds and, in the long run, these people could ill be spared. Nevertheless in 1874, at the height of their success, the agricultural Unions achieved a membership of 150,000, and, all through, Arch retained his pre-eminent position as leader and spokesman. However, trouble was at hand.

In 1873 a number of farmers in the Eastern Counties had threatened Union men with dismissal, and in the following year the process was repeated on a wider scale. By April over six thousand men had been locked out in Suffolk and north Essex for refusing to leave their Unions. The farmers solved their difficulties by employing 'blackleg' labour, but the Union men had to depend upon strike pay for their living. The Unions then enlisted the help of the towns and large sums of money were collected, but as harvest approached their members began to trickle back to work. In July the Union leaders stopped strike pay and advised the men to seek work elsewhere, thus ending all resistance to the lock-out. It was a serious blow to the whole Union movement, already weakened by internal dissension. Soon the depression in agriculture caused wages to fall, and Union membership declined. The 'National' dropped from 55,000 in 1877 to 15,000 in 1881, and to 4,250 in 1889. The 'Federal' Unions also broke up, and although there was a short resurgence in the late 1880s, most Union activity was over by the end of the century. Arch himself retired, an old and disappointed man, and many of the early pioneers either emigrated or gave up. But the first burst of Union activity had accomplished something. It had won several practical victories and it had proved the value of combination and self-help among the labourers. Also, some of the social legislation described earlier was directly due to Union agitation. The subsequent history of the Trades Union movement in the countryside was one of gradual reconstruction. At first the leadership devolved upon George Edwards, a farm worker who had been taught to read and write by his wife. In 1906, at the age of fifty-six, he started a new Union in East Anglia, which made some headway. Eventually he was joined by others, and after exchanging the Liberal for the Socialist interest in Parliament, two principal Unions were built up, serving the entire country, later to be known as *The National Union of Agricultural Workers*, and the agricultural section of *The Transport and General Workers' Union*. These two bodies now have a large membership and an assured position.

Until 1916 the fortunes of the agricultural labourer improved but very slowly. His wages were still less than £1 a week, but the Old Age Pension Act of 1909 assured him a pittance on retirement, and the National Health Insurance Act of 1911 assisted him in times of sickness. Ever since Rider Haggard's report in 1902, there had been signs of a limited recovery in farming, mainly due to the development of dairying and of grass; but the outbreak of the First World War had little immediate effect upon the pattern of agriculture and country life. An increasing number of farm workers left the land for the armed forces, but it was not until December 1916, when the County Executive Committees were set up, that the Government showed any real concern for increased food production. Soon, intensive U-boat warfare caused a desperate shortage of food, and in 1917 the Corn Production Act was passed which empowered the Board of Agriculture to enforce the ploughing up of pasture and the intensive cultivation of arable land for a period of six years. In return, guaranteed prices for corn were secured to the farmers, and this dual policy of compulsion and incentive did in fact obtain much of the extra food required. As to labour, the loss in personnel was partly offset by the employment of volunteers, of soldiers, schoolboys, and women in large numbers. Equally important was the setting up of Central and District Wages Boards, which regulated the hours of work and fixed a minimum wage. After this wages rose quickly, and by 1920 they were little short of 50s. a week.

In that year the Agriculture Act was passed, which superseded the Corn Production Act, withdrew State control over cultivation, continued the guarantee of grain prices, retained the Wages Boards, and adjusted once more the relations of landlord and tenant, particularly in regard to the payment of compensation for disturbance. All this was statesmanlike provision, a remarkable contrast to the depression days of Free Trade. However, it was not to last. It soon appeared that home agriculture was only to be tolerated so long as world food prices remained high. Once these fell, all the guarantees were thrown overboard, and Protection, at the very moment it was needed, abandoned. In 1921 the Agriculture Act, after eight months' life, was repealed, and the familiar processes were repeated. Arable farming went to pieces, and the land tumbled back to grass. Wages, no longer under the care of Wages Boards, dropped sharply, and by 1923 they were down to 30s. a week or less. There followed, naturally enough, an exodus of labour from the land, and the number of farm workers in England and Wales declined from 612,000 in 1921 to 511,000 in 1939.

In due course, however, a measure of protection for agriculture was reintroduced, but empirically, in the form of palliatives. In 1924 Wages Boards, in a modified form, were brought back, with the result that by the beginning of the Second World War basic rates had risen to about 35s. for a 50-hour week. Sugar-beet and wheat were subsidized; Marketing Boards were set up – some soon to be discarded, others, such as the Milk Marketing Board, to be retained; land improvement schemes by tile draining, piped water, and lime spreading were extended; agricultural land was de-rated, and tithe charges adjusted and amortized. Nevertheless the basic problem remained unsolved. So long as the national economy was founded upon the principle of exchanging manufactured goods for raw material and quantities of cheap food, English agriculture stood little chance either of finding a fair market for its output or of improving its own efficiency. In meeting this difficulty partial Protection was very little better than Free Trade; indeed the situation remained virtually unaltered until the Second World War, when fundamental changes were forced upon the whole structure of the nation's trade.

In the period between the two wars the English countryside was suffering from a social as well as an economic malady – the consequence of discouragement, exploitation, and neglect. The surface area of cultivable ground was heavily reduced by the lavish development of land. Not only were large areas of potential farmland actually abandoned – left to the sovereignty of thistles, thickets, and undergrowth, but great stretches of territory, including some of the best soil in the country (e.g. the Thames valley) were invaded by the builder. In the absence of any effective land-use policy, towns, large and small, expanded irresponsibly in every direction. Long spindly fingers of villas, filling stations, and roadhouses were pointed right into the heart of the country, awarding the new householders neither the advantages of the town nor the solace of the countryside. Factories were planted wherever land was accessible and cheap, with little regard either to social or to economic consequences. Besides this, parts of the countryside quickly assumed the nature of a playground – a place to relax in, not to work and live in.

In this way villages were often ruthlessly despoiled both in their physical appearance and in their character as communities. Country people, so long affected by economic depression, began to lose faith in their own prospects and in their own institutions. Sons and daughters had long been departing into industry, and their departure was now encouraged. The squire had become a syndicate or a manufacturer or an absentee; the parson was a poor man with the relics of a position; the schoolmaster, the craftsman, the shopkeeper, and many of the stalwarts of village life were dead or mere ghosts of their former selves. It seemed, in 1939, that the force of country life, as represented by the community of the village, was spent.

PART TWO

Elements of the Village

I

The Physical Element

THE appearance of an English village, often beautiful, always varied, is the result of continuous historical change; it is rarely the product of any single period or person. And although its beauty is difficult to analyse, yet it is possible to isolate some of those features which contribute, individually and collectively, to its existence.

SITE AND FORM

Clearly, all settlements must have a physical origin. In pre-historic times when the low-lying lands were covered with scrub, forest, or marsh, there was a tendency to populate either the hill-tops and plateaux, which were dry, accessible, and easy to defend, or the river banks where navigation presented no difficulties. Gradually, as implements and methods of tillage improved, the jungle was reduced and cultivation crept down the slopes into the valleys; and habitations multiplied upon the lower ground where the presence of shelter, water, and deeper soil became prime considerations. Thus proximity to, say, a spring or a wood was a frequent cause for settlement, and today many vil-lages reveal, through their names, a purely topographical origin. Later, as intercourse sprang up between communities, sites were adopted for commercial and other reasons; at a cross-roads, for instance, where tolls might be levied upon travellers, or a market set up to serve the immediate neighbourhood. Again, what was once a clearing in the forest, or a collection of squatters' huts, may have grown quite quickly into a prosperous village, owing to the foundation of a castle or an abbey, or the development of an industry.

Once the site was chosen, the influence of place was by no means at an end. The lie of the ground and outstanding natural features, such as a stream or a hill or a clump of trees, would all dictate the eventual form of the village. Where possible, compactness was the rule, for all members of the community had to be within walking distance of their work in the fields or with the cattle; or, if already at work, to be within sight and sound of home in case of need. In more civilized times this principle still held good. The houses stood close together, not far from the church, for centuries the only centre of social life, while the open fields and strips lay outside. Out of these limitations of place, two basic village forms arose, the *street* and the *square*, of which the former remains the commoner and the more rudimentary of the two. Until recently the *street* was no longer than that required by convenience and common sense; nor was it, of necessity, a mere monotonous string of houses lining the sides of the road. There was a certain feeling for landscape, visible in the planting of the trees, or in the separation of the houses from the road by a broad green verge, or again in the careful siting of the chief buildings, such as the inn or the church. Nor was lateral development precluded, and an occasional by-road to field or farm did not detract from the general pattern. Examples of this formation can clearly be recognized in a multitude of villages, one of which, Coxwold in Yorkshire, is illustrated on the next page.

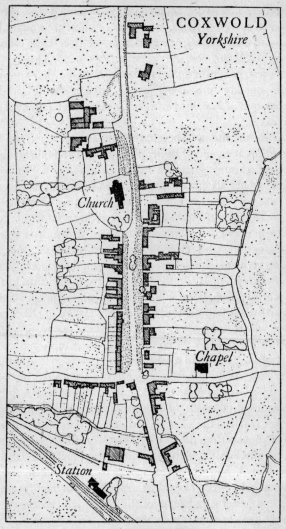

FIG. 6. — *A Street Village*

The *square* has many variations; in fact, any arrangement of buildings sited on more than one side of an open space may be so termed. In this way triangular, rectangular,

FIG. 7. — *A Square Village*

or oblong forms can be discerned, the general mass of the village circumscribing a green, a pond, or a market place. Markets nowadays are usually confined to country towns, but in the past many villages had weekly sales of cattle and goods, and in some cases this accounts for their 'square' shape today. Also, in the troubled Border country, where defence had always to be considered, the *square* is the traditional form. In this the church played an important part as a strong refuge for man and beast, with a command post and a look-out in the tower. The example shown on page 101 is Heighington in Durham.

However, since no rules can ever be dogmatically applied to the English countryside, it would be foolish to confine every village within either of these categories. A few conform absolutely, particularly those planned by landowners and others in the eighteenth and nineteenth centuries as estate or company villages. The majority approximate to one form or the other, or are a combination of both, and the residue cannot be classified at all. Coastal villages, for instance, are a subject by themselves, and apart from the fact that they usually radiate from the harbour, they are not open to generalization.

ARCHITECTURE — BUILDING MATERIALS

Until recently nearly everything built in the country, and certainly all cottages, farmsteads, and village buildings, were composed of local materials. The reason for this is plain. Since roads were rudimentary and navigable waterways comparatively rare, the haulage of stone, bricks, or timber over long distances was, before the nineteenth century, virtually impossible. It was also unnecessary, for each district in England had its own source of material and skill, and this fact has largely contributed to the astonishing variety of domestic architecture still found about the countryside. The map on page 104 gives a general clue to those geological resources immediately available for building. No attempt has been made to make a detailed survey of rock and soil structures, for this would merely result in a complex diagram quite outside the scope of this book. Nevertheless, in the general pattern that arises, the influence of geology can be clearly traced, and in one region after another the character of the villages is, in part, defined by the nature of the subsoil.

It will be seen that the natural materials used for building include a variety of quarried stone, granite, chalk, flints, sand, and wood. Clay is the chief component of brick, and often it is the essential foundation of timber as well. Earth must also be mentioned, for, as 'cob', it has been frequently used to make walls. As for roofing, stone, slate, clay (for tiles), and thatch (from straw or reed) are the commonest materials. Few of these are exclusive to any one area, for variations and intrusions abound in all parts of the country, especially where there are superficial deposits of clay and sand; and it must be emphasized that the limitations and advantages of local resources and technique have been largely neutralized since the Industrial Revolution. At the same time, the following summary, which should be read in conjunction with the map, will indicate the approximate trend of geological and architectural change.

ARCHITECTURE — EARLY CONSTRUCTION AND STYLE

Building construction in England was from the first a continuous evolutionary process; that is to say, one technical innovation grew out of another, and nearly every new style was an extension or development of an old one. Very little took root that was not related to the past, a state of affairs due, possibly, to the geographical separation of the country from the Continent. Of village building this was especially true. In the earliest times there were two general

GEOLOGICAL SKETCH MAP OF ENGLAND SHOWING AREAS OF BUILDING MATERIAL

KEY TO MAP

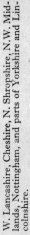

The northern counties, N.W. Yorkshire, E. Lancashire, down to the Peak District of Derbyshire.

Here, apart from small zones of sandstone and granite, carboniferous limestone is the dominant material. This produces a tough grey block, often with reddish or brown tints, somewhat rude and forbidding in character. Indeed this dour quality permeates not only the stone walls and slate roofs, but also the shapes of all the northern houses and the conditions of life in general.

W. Lancashire, Cheshire, N. Shropshire, N.W. Midlands, Nottingham, and parts of Yorkshire and Lincolnshire.

Here sandstone, marl, and millstone (or moorstone) grit are dominant. Millstone grit has a harsh grey colour akin to carboniferous limestone, and lies below extensive moorlands and peat beds. Red and grey sandstone has been widely used for building right through the northern part of this area, especially in Cheshire, Derby, and Nottingham, while farther south timber is prevalent, in association with both brick and stone.

A belt of country from E. Yorkshire across central England to Gloucestershire, thence southwards to Purbeck in Dorset.

Apart from the grey carboniferous limestone of the Mendip Hills, south of Bristol, the whole area is dominated by oolitic and liassic limestone. The former is a softer, lighter stone, that hardens and mellows under exposure, and is the substance of the architectural beauty of the Cotswolds. In the N.E., the limestone is found in conjunction with iron deposits

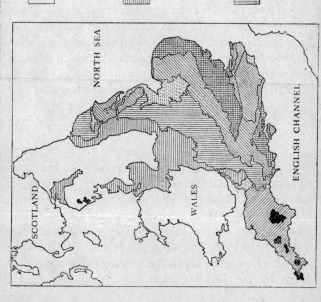

and other harder rocks. This change is reflected in the darker, duller colours of the stone-built houses, which are less attractive than, though structurally similar to, the Cotswold buildings.

Two outlying areas, north and south of the R. Humber, and a belt of country stretching from N. Norfolk, through the Chilterns to Berkshire, Hampshire, and Dorset. Thence eastwards to Kent, surrounding the clay area of the Weald.

These are the chalk districts which, like the soft limestone country, produce a pleasant and distinctive type of building. In Wiltshire and parts of Berkshire and Hampshire there is a quantity of sarsens (large sandstone boulders left behind by erosion on the surface of the ground) which serve excellently for cornerstones, lintels, and footings, and these are evident in many of the older cottages and barns. Sarsens too are in the majority among the monoliths of Avebury and Stonehenge. In the Weald area of Sussex and Kent there is a vast deposit of clay, at one time heavily afforested. This has slowly been cleared by the shipbuilders, and ironworkers who used charcoal for smelting, and the area is now mostly converted to agriculture. The clay, however, has given rise to brick and timber buildings, with plain tile or pantile roofs. Elsewhere thatch from corn straw or Norfolk reed is the natural roofing in 'chalk country'.

A belt of country stretching from N.E. Norfolk and Suffolk, southwards to Essex, London, Middlesex, and N. Kent, and westwards to Berkshire. In addition both sides of Southampton Water, and part of the Isle of Wight (which also has chalk formations).

These districts are characterized by large deposits of clay, sand, and gravel, and by a quantity of timber. Variations of use and technique are considerable, but the predominant house-building material is brick, with timber for framework. The fact, however, that London itself is largely built of brick is no sure clue to the surrounding geology, for the majority of buildings are less than a hundred years old, a period in which the transport of materials has greatly developed. Nevertheless traditional methods can still be found, especially in the Eastern Counties, where colour-washing and plastering with lime are evident, for both decorative and protective purposes.

The Fenland districts of Yorkshire, Lincolnshire, Cambridgeshire, Norfolk, Somerset, and Romney Marsh.

The general absence of local building materials in these districts has necessitated their importation from elsewhere. For this reason bricks and tiles, which are easy to handle, have usually been used.

Parts of Somerset and the whole of Devon and Cornwall.

Here there is a confusing variety of rock, about which it is difficult to generalize. In W. Somerset and E. Devon there is a large stretch of red sandstone and marl, and this gives rise to warm-tinted buildings in the towns and villages. On Exmoor and the north Devon coast the land loses its rich colours, although in certain places the red reappears. Southward lies a large carboniferous territory with pockets of granite, the largest belonging to Dartmoor, about 200 square miles in extent. Granite also occurs in Cornwall, particularly in altered form as china clay. Slates abound for roofing.

Granite is indicated thus.

methods of construction. One produced huts with a cir-
cular wooden framework, thatched over with wattle, clay,
or straw, the whole set round a central hearth of stones.
Such were the dwellings of the lake villages near Glastonbury (see page 22); but owing to its obvious structural
limitations the method was never developed. The alternative was the starting-point of most other rural building,
and consisted, in its elements, of two pairs of forked poles

FIG. 8. — *Primitive Cruck House*

or crucks, set up some distance apart, and linked by a horizontal ridge pole. Against this, rafters were secured, and
thatched over to provide a continuous roof line from the
ridge pole to the ground. The open ends were then filled
up, leaving space for an entrance. (See Fig. 8, above.)
This, too, was the form of construction later developed by
the Saxons, who employed stronger materials and greatly
enlarged the design. By that time the crucks had become
curved tree trunks securely settled upon foundation stones.
Instead of standing on the ground, the rafters now rested
upon horizontal lengths of timber, called wall-plates,

which, in turn, were supported by projecting tie-beams, that braced each pair of crucks. (See Fig. 9, below.) This allowed for a low wall between the roof and the ground and gave more room to the interior of the house. The internal length was standardized at about 16 feet, sufficient to stand four oxen abreast, the whole unit being known as a bay, a technical term freely used during succeeding centuries for describing and taxing property.

Wall plate

Tie beam

FIG. 9. – *Cruck Development*

In the majority of Saxon farmsteads humans and animals were housed in one or more bays under a single roof, although the 'house-part' was firmly barred off from the byre by a wall or a threshold or both. (See Fig. 10, page 108.) Under the Normans this system died out, and, while peasants and their families continued to share their living rooms with the small stock, the cattle and the horses were given separate lodging. Since they were flimsily built none of the early village houses has come down to us, but in the larger buildings made of stone, such as castles or churches, it is still possible to recognize the 'bay' principle. However,

about the end of the fourteenth century, stronger materials
were being freely used for cottages and other small dwellings. At that time the cottage was still a single-storey building of one bay. This bay or hall was rarely lengthened, for

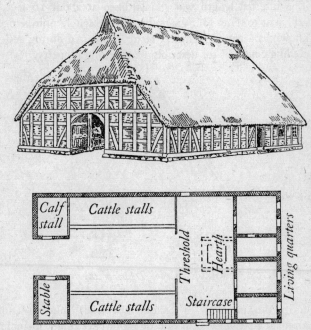

FIG. 10. — *Prototype of Saxon Farmhouse*

although another pair of crucks could easily have been put
up, it would probably have involved a higher tax assessment.
Instead, offshoots or 'outshuts' were added to any of the
four walls of the house — lean-to constructions reached by
an outside or inside door, and used for bedrooms or a but-
tery (where food and cooking utensils were kept) or even
for a privy. (See Fig. 11, page 109). Sometimes upper floors

were inserted above these additions, the hall remaining open to the roof. This was a common method of converting a

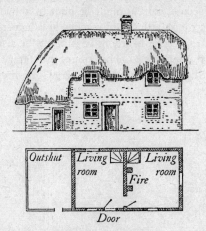

FIG. 11. — *Outshut Development in an existing Two-storeyed Cottage*

FIG. 12. — *H Construction*

cottage into a small farmhouse, or on a larger scale of converting a feudal hall into a manor house. The result was a rectangular building that resembled the letter H, containing a central hall between two two-storeyed extensions, the latter gabled or enclosed under one roof line. (See Fig. 12, page 109.) Alternatively, if only a small addition was needed, a second storey might be built in above the hall, and from a rough attic room reached by a ladder this later became a respectable bedroom with access by a staircase.

In many other ways, the interior of the cottage displayed an interesting and logical development. The fireplace, for

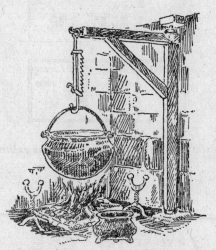

FIG. 13. — *Fireplace and Cooking Crane*

instance, originated as a hearth of flat stones laid in the centre of the hall, the smoke filtering through the roof as best it could, possibly assisted by a rough funnel of wood or wattle. Chimneys proper, built of brick or stone, were a sixteenth-century improvement and it was then that the fireplace came into its own. For cooking, a crane or a plain iron bar was installed above the hearth, and from this were suspended long hooks for kettles and pots. (See Fig. 13, above.) Beside this a baking oven was built, and screens erected on either side to protect the company from draughts.

Likewise, the window evolved from a mere 'wind-hole' into an opening with a shutter, or a frame of plaited osiers. (See Fig. 14, left.) These early windows were very small, partly because they were difficult to make, and partly because the houses were sufficiently ventilated by ill-fitting timbers and doors; the chief problem was the admission of light. Glass, although an early invention, was for long scarce and expensive, and did not come into general use until the end of the sixteenth century. Even then, owing to

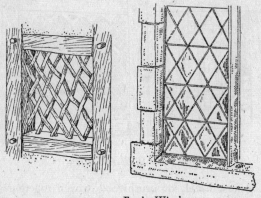

FIG. 14. — *Early Windows*

technical limitations, only 'crown' or 'bottle' glass was made, and this was cut into small diamond-shaped panes, fitted into a leaden framework on the old lattice principle, and strengthened by vertical or horizontal bars, known respectively as mullions and transoms. (See Fig. 14, right.) Later still, iron casements were introduced that opened and shut, and these were succeeded by wooden casements and frames, and by sliding sash windows.

TIMBER FRAMING

By the middle of the sixteenth century the cruck was being replaced by the post-and-truss method of construction in most buildings with a timber framework. When a house was built, a hard foundation was first put down, and on top of this were laid horizontal beams of timber, socketed for upright posts. At first the distance between these posts was small, but as timber grew scarce the intervening panels became larger and squarer, and the in-filling of wattle and

FIG. 15. – *Wall In-Fillings*

daub (osiers, hazel, or brushwood woven together and plastered over with clay) replaced by bricks. (See Fig. 15, above.) The upper storey was similarly constructed and supported on joists which projected over the lower storey, a feature known as jettying; the object of this has been variously attributed to a desire on the part of the builder to gain space, to protect the ground wall from the weather, or to reinforce the superstructure by means of this cantilever construction. After some years, the upright posts were extended to run the whole distance from roof to foundation, and jettying was abandoned. Perhaps the greatest difference

between medieval and Elizabethan timbering was notice-
able in the method of supporting the roof. In the former the
wall-plates rested on the tie-beam; in the latter the system
was reversed, the tie-beam rested on the wall-plates, and
this transferred the weight more safely to the walls. (See
Fig. 16, below.) The oak framework was generally pre-
fabricated. The lengths were sawn or adzed, and num-
bered at the sawpit, then taken to the site, where they were
slotted and pinned together with oak pegs, and so erected.

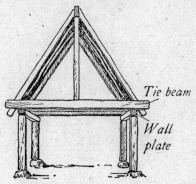

Tie beam

*Wall
plate*

FIG. 16. – *Transition from Cruck to Post-and-Truss*

House building of this kind was usually a communal
matter, for many hands were required, and the whole village joined in to complete the work. (See Fig. 17, page
114.)

The timber-framed building is found nearly everywhere
in England, but in quantity it is confined to certain recognizable regions, and in each of these it carries some further
mark of individuality. In the south and south-east, for instance, jettying is not the invariable rule, and the woodwork
is left unstained. In-filling with bricks is common, and
these are often left untreated; alternatively the whole wall

may be lime-washed or plastered, or hung with tiles. In East Anglia plastering or *pargetting* was the normal practice, a strikingly decorative art, displaying a wide variety of simple patterns scratched out with a comb or formal subjects worked up in bas-relief. (See Fig. 18, below.) Other variants in the south-east are colour-washing and

Floor joists jettied

FIG. 17. — *A Timber Frame*

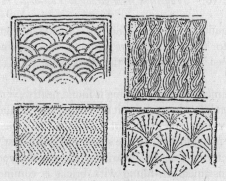

FIG. 18. — *Pargetting Patterns*

weather-boarding, the basic intention in each case being to preserve the framework and the in-filling from the elements. The other main region of timber-framing lies in the Midlands and along the Welsh border; particularly in the counties of Warwick, Worcester, Hereford, and in parts of Shropshire and Cheshire. Here jettying is frequent, the timbers are set wider apart, and much of the woodwork is decorated and darkened to contrast strongly with the whitened walls. (See Plate 6 b.)

BRICK

After the departure of the Romans, the art of brick-making seems to have died out in this country. Bricks eventually returned to favour with the Elizabethans, were imported from the Low Countries, and used, initially, in the eastern half of England. At first they were reserved for wall-filling and for chimneys, but, with the elaboration of the fire-place, bricks soon established a hold over all parts of the building. By the end of the seventeenth century solid brick construction was replacing timber in a wide field. Brick, it was found, had many advantages: it was fire and vermin proof, it was practical and easy to use, and, once the manufacture was understood, comparatively cheap. Ornament, too, was a possibility; for instance, by various methods of bonding, that is, laying 'headers' and 'stretchers' in different ways, or by using darker bricks for patterns. (See Fig. 19, page 116.) Similar results were obtained by combining brick and flints or brick and stone, although the latter is not always attractive. The development of towns during the eighteenth century popularized brick even further, and the devotion to classical form exerted in due course an influence on all village building. Cottages gained in simplicity and elegance, the windows were larger and better proportioned, and the general construction was altogether of a higher order. Indeed, most Georgian country buildings are finished and urbane; they no longer display the rough and tumble of their predecessors, when draughts and

FIG. 19. — *Brick Bonding*

smoke were taken as a matter of course. Latterly brick has become almost universal in use, to the great detriment of our rural building character. Once the railways had opened up the countryside, it became easier and cheaper to transport 30,000 or 130,000 bricks to, say, the Cotswolds, than to quarry the equivalent quantity of stone on the spot. Thus all through the Victorian era the individuality of building gradually declined, craftsmen in the specialized trades diminished, and the village lost its local homogeneity. Traditional brick building, however, is always attractive, and it still abounds in all the characteristic clay regions.

STONE

Owing to cost and to difficulty of handling, stone was originally reserved for buildings of importance, such as castles or churches. However, as the price of timber rose in relation to its scarcity, so stone came into its own, in the appropriate districts, for building of every sort. Architecturally the outstanding region is the Cotswolds where three centuries of economic prosperity based on wool, besides the presence of building material just below the surface of the ground, produced a style of remarkable beauty.

This beauty was emphasized by three things — the weathering properties of the oolitic limestone, the high standard of the mason's work, and the fact that all buildings from churches to cottages were built in a similar style and material. In this way a harmony was achieved that has been rarely equalled elsewhere in the English countryside. Other villages in the limestone belt approximate to the Cotswold style but do not arrive at the same perfection. In the north-east the proximity of ironstone produces a darker and less

FIG. 20. — *Stone-built House in the Cotswolds*

attractive colour; in the south, although the rich Bath and Portland stone produces some charming villages in Somerset, Wiltshire, and Dorset, there is not the same technical finish. Again, in the north, the toughness of the mountain limestone precludes most ornament which, in the softer stone country, goes far to produce a sympathetic exterior. Where, however, the stone can be cut in large blocks, then a certain massive simplicity is gained by the use of ashlar, or squared stone, especially for quoins, lintels, and window-dressings. Sometimes a whole wall has been fitted together with ashlar bedded dry, but generally the building is completed with rubble stones, roughly coursed and mortared. In Cornwall and Devon, where from earliest times buildings have been erected of granite, the block has been disguised with coats of whitewash or lime, and this improves both the appearance and the resistance of the walls. The sandstone villages of the south-west and the north Midlands also have a warmer character, but this is due more to the colour of the stone than to any architectural refinement such as may be found in the Cotswolds. (See Plate 8 a.)

BRIEF NOTES ON OTHER BUILDING MATERIALS

Flints are generally found in combination with other materials – with chalk in Berkshire, Buckinghamshire, and Wiltshire, with brick in the clay districts of Hampshire, Sussex, and Kent, and with both chalk and brick in parts of East Anglia. Here 'galleting' or 'garneting' is practised, a local method of pressing flint chips into the wet mortar that produces a pleasant piebald pattern. (See Plate 8 b.)

Cob is a mixture of soil, dung, straw, and water, rammed into a solid consistency. For long life it should rest upon a solid foundation of stone, be covered with a thatch roof, and coated with lime or tar. If these conditions are satisfied it lasts for centuries, as the cob villages of the south-west still testify. (See Plate 9.)

Chalk, where used alone, is not really satisfactory, except when hardened off into square blocks known as 'clunch'. Sometimes it has been mixed up with straw and water to form a substance akin to cob, but generally it is combined with bricks, flints, or stone, and washed over with lime.

Clay Lump is, in effect, a primitive form of brickmaking, practised in the past in some eastern counties. The clay is dug out of the ground and prepared 'cob fashion'. It is then moulded into large bricks and left out to dry. It is usually associated with flint or brick in wall construction and, like chalk and cob, benefits considerably from a coat of lime.

ROOFING

Roofs have as many regional variations as walls. In many village buildings the roof line finishes in a pointed gable, but by the eighteenth century the 'hip' (a triangular slope at either end) had become popular. Another variant is the 'curb', found principally in East Anglia; this divides the roof in two and bestows more space upstairs. In general, pitch is determined by the material used, for thatch and tiles can be secured almost vertically, while slates and stone require a flatter angle. (See Fig. 21, page 120.)

Stone slats or *slabs* are quarried in the same way and in the same districts as stone for walls. The stone itself is selected and exposed to frost, which loosens the natural layers. These are then split open and sorted into appropriate sizes. In the Cotswolds stone roofing is still a live craft and a whole range of curious names are given to the types of slat used – Spots, Bachelors, Farwells, etc. The labour, however, is extremely specialized and expensive, and normally stone roofs are not an economic proposition. Instead, concrete imitations have been substituted on a number of small houses, with very fair results. Elsewhere stone slats are coarser and less attractive, while in parts of the north large heavy slabs are the rule; but these require stronger and flatter roofs to support them.

Thatch is in constant use, in all parts of the south and east, and there are still a fair number of skilled craftsmen who maintain the ancient trade. Thatching is of two kinds, straw and reed, and each is capable of much local variation. Wheat or rye produces the best thatching straw, but its durability is badly impaired by threshing. Another drawback is its vulnerability to fire and to the inroads of birds, although both can to a certain extent be countered; the former by treatment with an alum solution, the latter by laying wire netting over the roof after the thatch has been laid. Straw is more pliable than reed and tends to adapt itself more readily to hipped roofs, curved dormers, and the like. Reed lasts longer, gives a finer finish, and is worked up in the Eastern Counties into remarkable schemes of decoration.

Slates abound in the south-west and in the north-west, and have an attractive range of tones. However, the drab

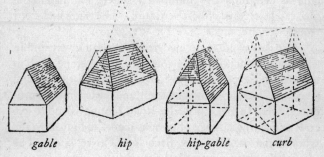

gable   *hip*   *hip-gable*   *curb*

FIG. 21. – *Methods of Roof Construction*

machine-made Welsh slates are less pleasing, and their popularity for roofing suburban villas and council cottages has given them, aesthetically, a bad name.

Tiles. Like bricks, tiles were a comparatively late introduction into the English countryside; and as an alternative to thatch they matched brick walls in most of the clay

FIG. 22. — *Principles of Roof and Wall Tiling*

regions. Latterly, however, tiles have gained in popularity, and have been used to replace old thatch or stone slats. There are two principal varieties — the plain straight tile and the S-shaped pantile. (See Fig. 22, above.)

CONCLUSION — THE SETTING

Site, form, architecture, these three constitute the physical element of the village. Yet there is a fourth factor, less tangible, but no less important, which to some extent is implicit in the first three — setting. This might be described as 'the relationship of the village to its immediate neighbourhood', which, it must be emphasized, is rarely a completely fortuitous one. The attractions of the English countryside are due as much to artifice as to Nature, or at least to the results of artifice; and this is evident in that before the Great Enclosures the land had quite a different appearance to the one we know now. Then there were few hedges or plantations, and no ordered pattern of field and farmstead as characterizes England to native and foreign eyes; only vast expanses of wood and waste, intersected by settlements, by the open fields and meadows, and by an occasional enclosed property. By 1820 the landscape had been completely changed, for Enclosure and the technical advances of agriculture had already had their effect. Instead of all clustering within the curtilage of the village (a form of settlement suited to primitive agriculture and conditions of life) the farmsteads were now replanted in the open countryside, each the capital of its own holding. The fields themselves varied greatly in size and shape; many followed the old irregular boundaries of the strips, others had been carved rectangular fashion out of unbroken land, fenced off by quickset hedges or earthen banks or low stone walls. The pattern was deliberate.

There was, however, another important consideration. Ever since the seventeenth century there had been a growing desire on the part of landowners to plant trees. This had a twofold purpose – to supply timber for ship and house building, charcoal burning, and the general needs of commerce, and to satisfy a purely aesthetic impulse. This impulse had had its origins in an earlier movement for creating gardens, particularly those of formal design attached to large country houses. Gradually the gardens had been extended and embellished by avenues, prospects, and plantations, some on a grandiose scale, and 'landscaping' came to be regarded as an art, practised by skilled practitioners such as Kent and Capability Brown. However, patrons and practitioners were not confined to one section of society, and the distinction bestowed upon the general countryside by the myriad hedgerow trees and copses is the result of widespread plantation by yeoman farmers and others, who had been fired by the same impulse. With the village itself the story is not dissimilar. A number were entirely rebuilt and replanned by landowners, who had their eye upon the setting, and in many cases the church or other prominent building had been sited and designed with an aesthetic end in view. In general, however, it was the gradual domestication of Nature, allied to the practical requirements of an agricultural life, based on purely local resources, that produced the physical harmony which still distinguishes the English village.

Unfortunately the acceleration of industrialism and the spread of urban influences over the countryside during the last hundred and fifty years have destroyed this innate sense of setting among all classes of people. Good taste, for long the unconscious product of tradition, was replaced by the meanness of expediency, and by purely utilitarian considerations. In the ordinary run of nineteenth- and twentieth-century village building, cheapness was the first concern, but even where it was not, the magic touch had been lost. By itself, of course, cheapness is no criterion, since the majority of old cottages had been put up at very small cost. The fault lay, possibly, in mechanizing (and imitating with the machine) essentially manual methods of production, in lowering the quality of the article produced, and in supplying goods in such large quantities that all individuality was suppressed. Bricks are a case in point. It is only necessary to look at rural railway stations, and at the brick houses that lead up to them, to see that this is true. There have been, from time to time, reactions against the prevailing materialism. William Morris and his friends were the embodiment of one such movement. Unfortunately the solution that they offered — the rejection of the machine and an artificial renewal of the handicrafts — was impracticable. Certainly it did nothing to restore the true relationship between the community and the countryside.

In fact, the problem went far deeper than mere technicalities. The growth of industrialism and the consequent disruption of rural life was the real cause of this disharmony – physical appearances were merely the symptoms. This became more evident as the twentieth century proceeded. Agriculture seemed permanently distressed, rural crafts all but disappeared, and villages either decayed or were ruthlessly exploited for the benefit of the towns. In such circumstances, it is not surprising that the architectural and the other physical traditions were lost. Renewal is a matter of the regeneration of the entire rural community, and that can come about only through the agency of a conscious and deliberate piece of planning.

2

The Industrial Element

AGRICULTURE has rarely been the sole source of employment in the village. At all times the countryman has had need of tools and tackle for his trade, quite apart from products essential to existence, such as clothes, furniture, and utensils. Thus in early years the majority of agricultural implements, and of personal and household goods, were made by members of the family, at home and upon the farm. The women, for instance, sewed skins, spun wool and wove it into cloth, or they kneaded and fired clay pots; the men carpentered ashen rakes and harrows, plaited osiers into baskets, or hewed timber for their hovels. Even so, specialization was an early development. In prehistoric Britain, first the flint knappers, then the bronze, gold, and iron or black smiths were soon evident. They made many of the implements with which primitive man hunted, fought battles, and won a living from the earth; also the jewellery which adorned his womenfolk and marked his status in society.

Indeed it was the smith who laid the foundations of industrial and economic progress; and this was due not only to the potentialities of his products, but also to the fact that extensive organization was required to keep him at work. For example, the raw material had to be located and extracted from the earth; and, however superficial the deposits, mining and the preparation of the ore involved considerable labour and skill. Secondly, once the smith was established at any distance from his source of supply, communications had to be improved and transport developed.

There then followed all the technical problems of manufacture, and the question of the disposal of the finished article. The development of these various aspects of the metal industry influenced the manufacture and exchange of the majority of the other industrial goods and services. This applied to the production both of tools for use by other craftsmen (without which they could not carry on

FIG. 23. — *Blacksmith's Shop*

their separate trades) and of goods necessary to the general life of the community. Iron, in particular, gave birth to the most important developments. It was the iron axes of the Celts and later of the Belgae that reduced the primeval forests of the plains. It was the heavy Belgic iron plough that first bit deeply into the soil and turned it over. The Romans, too, owed much of their superiority to their use of iron, both in war and in agriculture. And although the highly developed villa estates had largely been abandoned by the end of the fourth century (and, one supposes, most of the skilled processes that they supported), it is certain that the use of iron survived. Indeed the Saxons employed it on a larger scale than ever before, particularly in the reclamation of forest areas, and in the tillage of the stiffer soils of the valleys. In every sense, therefore, the smith must be regarded as the 'master craftsman', a position of outstanding importance in early rural society.

By the time of the Norman Conquest, the range of rural crafts had been extended and consolidated. In the larger villages were to be found the smith, the carpenter (and wheelwright), the tinker, the potter, and the miller; some services may have been performed by travelling craftsmen who worked over a territory where settlements were scattered and small. Most other skilled work (now regarded as specialized) remained part of the general repertory of the peasant and his family. Under feudalism, which was a patriarchal form of society, the rural craftsman had his allotted place like the other orders. He had a cottage and a small enclosure, possibly a few strips in the open fields, and rights over the commons. In certain manors, pastures were set aside for the particular use of craftsmen and officials; this accounts for field names such as Smithsham, Constable's Field, Parson's Hill, etc.; but the total holding of a craftsman would never have been large, else farmwork would have interfered with the practice of his trade. Indeed he was usually exempt from the labour services incumbent upon the villein and the other unfree tenants; instead, he paid his rent to the manor in the form of goods or services relevant to his profession. But ultimately, as a result of the economic changes accelerated by the Black Death, he was able to discharge all such obligations in cash.

An insight into the wide scope of country crafts at the end of the Middle Ages is provided by Thomas Tusser, the sixteenth-century agricultural writer mentioned in Part One. In one of his compositions entitled *Husbandly Furniture*, he refers to not less than one hundred and fifty tools, implements, and utensils essential to the farm; in another, *The Good Housewive's Day*, he lists a multitude of domestic accomplishments, of which many would now be classified as crafts. But industrial production was no longer confined to isolated craftsmen or to the farmwife. In certain parts of the countryside, village trades were mutually dependent. Thus the need for ships, boats, and tackle gave work to sack-, sail-, and rope-makers, as well as to the boat-builders in coastal and riverside neighbourhoods. Similarly, cart-wrights, wheelwrights, and harness-makers tended to establish themselves in villages situated beside the highways. In some places industrial work was dominated by the presence of natural resources and the ability to exploit them. Thus there was surface coal mining in Northumberland and the Midlands; iron smelting in Kent, Sussex, the Forest of Dean, and in the Furness district of Lancashire; lead mining in Derbyshire, Cumberland, and the Mendips; tin mining in Cornwall; and stone quarrying in many parts, but specifically in Dorset, Gloucestershire, and Somerset.

The most important medieval industry was that connected with the manufacture of wool and, as already stated, was concentrated in the main in the West Country, in East Anglia, and in the West Riding of Yorkshire. Here the labour was subdivided into not less than a dozen processes, each the responsibility of a different set of craftsmen or craftswomen. This was the cradle of both the highly organized craft gilds and of free capitalist enterprise. The former was an urban system whereby, in the case of wool, the material was worked up and sold by one craftsman to another as each process was completed. The latter was a rural development by which the merchant or factor, who

1(a). Stonehenge (1.1)

1(b). Celtic Fields, Burderop Down, Wiltshire (1.1)

2(a). Erecting Combe Gibbet, 1950 (II.5)

2(b). Avebury (I.1)

To the Constables of the City and County of EXON,
and to every of them; and also to all Constables, and other Officers,
whom it may concern to receive and convey; and to the Church
Wardens, Chapel-Wardens, or Overseers, of the Poor of the
Parish ———— of *Brushford* ————
in the County of *Somerset* ———— or either of them
to receive and obey,

EXON, } WHEREAS *Elizabeth Budd Singlewoman* ———
to wit. }

apprehended in the Parish of *Saint John* within the
said City and County of EXON, as a Rogue and Vagabond
and convicted..
......................., wandering abroad, lodging in the open Air, ...g a
good Account of ——— and upon Examination of the
said *Elizabeth Budd*
taken upon Oath before me, one of his Majesty's Justices of the
Peace of and for the said City and County of EXON (which
Examination is hereunto annexed), it doth appear, that the Place of
the last legal Settlement of the said *Elizabeth Budd*

Ruth Chamberlain
Mayor

is in the Parish of *Brushford*
in the County of *Somerset*
These are therefore to require you the said Constables, some or one
of you, to convey the said Vagabond to the Parish of *St. Thomas the
Apostle* in the County of *Exon*, (that being the first Parish in the next
Precinct through which *she* ought to pass, in the direct Way to
the said Parish of *Brushford* ——— to which *she is* to
be sent) and deliver *her* to the Constable, or other Officer of
the said Parish of *St. Thomas the Apostle*, together with this Pass, and
a Duplicate of the said Examination, taking his Receipt for the same,
And the said Vagabond *is* to be thence conveyed on, according
to the Direction of the Statute in that Case lately made and provided,
to the said Parish of *Brushford*
there to be delivered to some Church-Warden, Chapel-Warden, or
Overseer of the Poor of the same Parish to be there provided for
according to Law. And you the said Church-Wardens, Chapel-
Wardens, and Overseers of the Poor, are hereby required to receive
her and provide for *her* as aforesaid. *And I do
hereby Certify that the said Vagrant hath been
Confined in the House of Correction for the Space of 7 days*
Given under my Hand and Seal this *1st* Day of
February ——— in the Year of our Lord 179 *9.*

3. Removal Order (II.3)

4. Typical enclosed country, Yorkshire (1:5)

5: A modern farm, Northamptonshire (1.7)

6(a). Victorian village building, at Bourton, Berkshire (1.6)

6(b). Black and White Timber Framing, Hereford (11.1)

7(a). Weatherboard, Tiling and a Curb Roof, Essex (11.1)

7(b). Pargetted House, Suffolk (11.1)

8(a). Chipping Campden, Glos. – A 'Wool' Village built of Limestone (11.1)

8(b). Brick, Flint and Thatch, Wiltshire (11.1)

9. Cob and Stone, Devon (II.1)

10(a). Cattle show (11.5)

10(b). Carnival (11.5)

11(a). Jordans Meeting House (11.4)

11(b). A village church (11.4)

12(a–d). Organ gallery, pews, screen, and parish chest in Brushford Church, Somerset (11.4)

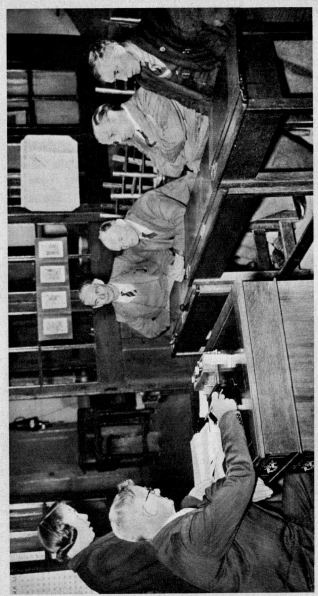

13. A Parish Council Meeting (11.3)

14(a). A Village Pub (11.5)

14(b). A Village School (11.4)

15(a). A Village Hall (11.5)

15(b). A Village Playing Field (11.5)

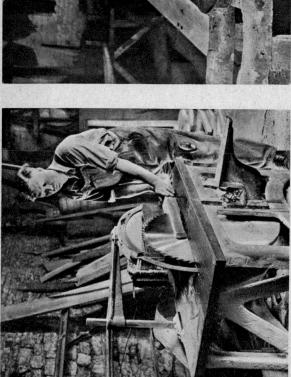

New and Old in Village Industry (11.2)

16(b). Preparing a Cart Wheel

16(a). Using a Mechanical Saw

owned the material from first to last, put it out for manufacture to village workers, to whom he paid wages. Occasionally the employees were congregated in a factory, as at the establishment of John Winchcombe (Jack o' Newbury) in the sixteenth century, but in the main they lived and worked at home. The craft gilds were essentially a medieval institution, flourishing in the thirteenth and fourteenth centuries, and directing all their energies towards a monopoly of trade. This characteristic was both a strength and a weakness. At its best it achieved high standards of work, much artistic beauty, and a social conscience among the members of the gilds. However, when commerce expanded during the fifteenth and sixteenth centuries, monopoly gradually degenerated into a narrow rigidity, which prevented the gilds from adapting themselves to the new circumstances of trade, and allowed them to be outstripped by capitalist concerns, less fettered by restrictions. In the textile trade, it resulted in the movement of industry from town to countryside; a movement accelerated by the development of worsted – woollen fabrics that did not require the thickening process known as fulling. Thus, in by-passing the fulling mill, hitherto the focus of woollen manufacture, the tendency towards dispersal was still further encouraged. At the same time the decline of the gilds did not mean that the craftsman who owned his own business was immediately superseded by the employer of paid labour. So long as the demands of trade could adequately be met by manual methods of production, the cottager, working for the factor, and the master-craftsman continued to exist side by side. Paradoxically enough, it was the cottage or domestic system, essentially a village concern, that anticipated modern industrial organization in that it lent itself to large-scale production. The urban gilds did not, and for that and other reasons they did not survive.

E.V.—5

At this stage there is no straightforward means of differentiating in technical terms between craft and industry. Both relied on manual skill, and while the former required few hands to produce an article or complete a process, the latter was nothing more than an alliance of mutually dependent handicrafts. However, once demand had begun to forge ahead of supply and exceed all the efforts of the hand-worker to meet it, then invention was stimulated and power-driven machines introduced. In this way industry, in the modern sense of the term, was established, and a gulf fixed between the village craftsman and the machine operative of the town. Of course, power itself was nothing new; it had existed since early days in the form of wind or water for driving corn and fulling mills, forge hammers, and the like; but it had always supplemented the human hand, not displaced it. The machine age began early in the eighteenth century, and at first mechanization was only a gradual process, both hand and machine operations existing simultaneously for many years. In the textile trade, for instance, spinning had lagged far behind the demands of the weavers, but in 1765 Hargreaves perfected his spinning jenny – a multi-spindle machine that could be hired and operated in the worker's cottage. Then in 1769 Arkwright patented a water-driven spinning frame – a real symptom of revolution, for it necessitated installation in a factory, and this anticipated the end of the domestic system.

These early factories were located for the most part beside hill streams in the north-west, but with the progress of invention, in particular the development of steam, hill sites became unnecessary, and industry began to conglomerate near the coalfields and in the towns. Indeed it was steam power, more than anything else, that set the seal on the handicraft industry of the countryside. One village trade after another disappeared or migrated north. Wool deserted East Anglia and the West. Iron smelting had already expired in the Kent and Sussex Weald, while a myriad small works, mills, and cottage industries, some with a national reputation, others serving purely local needs, were undercut and extinguished. Typical examples among many quoted by Lord Ernle in his book *English Farming, Past and Present** include hemp spinning, osier baskets, and reed matting in Bedfordshire, baize making in Essex, silk weaving near Canterbury, the velvet trade of Banbury, and the powder mills of Faversham and Deptford. In Cornwall, however, there was no decline, for there the steam-driven pumps of Thomas Newcomen and later those of Boulton and Watt made possible the deep mining of tin and copper; one case in which mechanization supplemented the human hand and preserved the life of an early craft.

The village, moreover, was becoming more accessible. The old local monopolies had not been difficult to maintain in view of the lack of good communication, and the intense local patriotism that resulted from isolation. All this began to disappear before the Turnpikes, the canals, the great trunk roads built by Thomas Telford and John Macadam, and after 1840 the railways – which were all opening up the countryside at a tremendous pace. On the other hand Enclosure and the revolution in arable farming widened the scope of some of the village crafts. The commercial exploitation of agriculture did not in the long run create unemployment, although its immediate impact was often a social disaster. Intensive methods of cultivation required as much labour as the open fields, while by 1800 at least new work was devolving upon the smith, the wheelwright, the thatcher, and other field tradesmen. Moreover, with the increase in field machinery, especially

*Longmans.

during the period of High Farming – say between 1850 and 1870 – new openings were being created for the rural engineer and the contractor. It was not until the late 1870s, the 1880s, and the 1890s, years of deep depression in agriculture, of which an account has already been given in Part One, that village crafts and industries began finally to fall away.

Among contemporary records there is a lively description of a village foundry, which appears in Alfred Williams' *Villages of the White Horse*.* It illustrates, among other things, how reluctantly and how stubbornly the trade was given up.

The village foundry has existed for nearly two centuries, and, though it is only a small place, it has sufficed for the immediate needs of the neighbourhood. It is chiefly repairs that are executed, and not new machinery made, though there are a few new implements constructed, and especially heavy farm waggons and carriages. Nearly every village of any importance had its foundry till a few years ago, and though the number has diminished there are still many to be met with here and there: there are no less than seven or eight within a radius of twelve miles of the village. It is true that the amount of work required of them has tragically fallen off of late years, but the owners and staff keep plodding away, with true rural grit, and the determination not to be utterly extinguished. Steam traction and ploughing sets provided them with much work and now they are on the decline the steam motor-lorry has come into being, and many of the larger village foundries are occupied with the manufacture of them.

The foundry at Chiseldon finds work in all for thirty-four hands. Of this number about half are mechanics employed in the worksheds, the others are engaged with steam-ploughing and threshing sets, steam-rolling the roads, and acting the part of hauliers. Twenty years ago the owners of the foundry at Swindon, four miles off, had fourteen sets of threshing tackle generally in

*Duckworth.

use, while today they have but two, and these not in very frequent demand.

The foundry staff proper includes the working manager — a fine type of village engineer, tall and square, with ruddy cheeks, bluff and hearty, and clever at his trade, having a practical knowledge of everything connected with his work, — two smiths, a boilermaker, three fitters and turners, a moulder, and three or four carpenters and waggon-builders. These occupy a small group of buildings connected together, and are able to see each other at work, to communicate with, and consult one another on various points, and to work co-operatively, which is impossible in the big factories of the towns.

The casting shed is a small stone-built place, long and narrow and ancient-looking; its walls are cracked with the great heat, and appear half ready to topple down. The floor is of sand, black with continual use in the frames, and there is a heap of it just inside the door waiting to be made up again; it is used many times over for moulds. The moulds are set in rows down the centre of the shed, and the small furnace, cylindrical in shape, stands near the outer wall. The blast for this is supplied by a small fan, driven from the main shafting. Before oil and steam engines were thought of, the blast was forced by machines impelled by horses, and also by human power, and the speed was multiplied with gear. In one corner is a tiny furnace, like a washer-woman's boiler, for drying the cores; and near by is a small pitlike place, used as a brass smelter. There is a small fire lit, and regulated by natural draught, which is sufficient for melting brass; iron and steel require a much more intense heat to reduce them to a liquid state.

The moulder is highly intelligent and very talkative. He lays particular stress on the value to be got from an experience of village foundries, where the workman is required to have a knowledge of many things. 'I worked in them big works five year, an' I can tell you, mister, you learns more outside at these small places in one twelvemonth than you would ther' in a lifetime. An' why? Cos they wunt let e learn nothin'. Ther's sheens for this, an' sheens for that; everything's cut an' dried, an' ther you be, slavin' like a nigger all yer time, at the same owl job, an' a girt fool at the end on't; an' if you got to move out anywher' else, you be no good at all; you don' know nothin'.'

Another classic of village industry is *The Wheelwright's Shop*[*] by George Sturt (who wrote under the pseudonym George Bourne), the biography of an old-established family business at Farnham in Surrey. When he started work as a young man in 1884 conditions had hardly altered since his grandfather's time. Quality and workmanship mattered most and all the custom was local.

Farmers rarely more than five miles away; millers, brewers, a local grocer or builder or timber-merchant or hop-grower – for such and no others did the ancient shop still cater, as it had done for nearly two centuries. And so we got curiously intimate with the peculiar needs of the neighbourhood. In farm-waggon or dung-cart, barley-roller, plough, water-barrel, or what not, the dimensions we chose, the curves we followed (and almost every piece of timber was curved) were imposed upon us by the nature of the soil in this or that farm, the gradient of this or that hill, the temper of this or that customer or his choice perhaps in horseflesh.

But the end of the story was familiar. Quite soon Sturt realized that owing to the absence of costing the shop was losing money on everything but repair work; in fact, none of the prices had been altered for generations. At the same time none of his men would lower their standards for the sake of turning out a cheaper vehicle and so maintain the trade. Theirs was the ancient spirit of craftsmanship which the Industrial Revolution had failed to change. Events, however, forced the issue, and in order to survive Sturt successfully introduced some machinery – 'a gas-engine, with saws, lathe, drill, and grind-stone. And this device, if it saved the situation, was (as was long afterwards plain) the beginning of the end of the old style of business, though it

[*] Cambridge University Press.

did just bridge over the transition to the motor-trade of the present time.' It was indeed the 'beginning of the end'. By 1900 it was already becoming clear that village craftsmen were facing extinction, and that survival depended, perhaps, upon one of two things: upon the fortuitous absence of competition by the machine, but this field was retracting every day: and upon limited mechanization of the kind described by George Sturt. This last offered considerable scope; it did not entirely displace manual skill, and it enabled rural products to be sold at competitive prices. However, only a minority were aware of these possibilities, and so the decline in rural industrial life continued apace.

On the other hand, for village commerce (as distinct from manufacture) the nineteenth century was a period of improvement. In the Middle Ages there were only three or four sources of retail trade other than barter: the itinerant merchant with his packhorse, the weekly market held in large villages or small towns, the seasonal Fair, and the village craftsman himself who was his own merchant, who bought or grew his raw material, and who sold as well as made his particular goods. In fact, the word 'shop' originally signified 'workshop', not merely a place of sale. These conditions continued almost unchanged right up to the Industrial Revolution. But with the improvement of communications, especially of the parish roads under the reformed highway administration of the mid nineteenth century, the countryside was laid open to outside suppliers. Soon retail shops were set up in villages, stocked by wholesalers in the town; few of them were specialized, most – although not all – were general or mixed stores, and that is still the case today. This was due to sound business reasons, for specialization demands a larger number of customers than can be supplied by one small area, such as a village. Likewise some country shopkeepers carried on more than one trade. Mr Jolson, for instance, owner of the Benfield stores in Adrian Bell's *Corduroy*,* was also a moneylender, and an arrangement of this sort made several professions economically possible. Moreover, until at least the twentieth century, most villages of size maintained a fair independence in such matters. For example, in 1868, Cassey's *Directory of Berkshire* records the village of Inkpen (population 748) as having two carriers, two cattle and horse dealers, one potter, one tailor, one bricklayer, two shoemakers, one basket-maker, two bakers, two carpenter-wheelwrights, one blacksmith, two innkeepers, and one general shopkeeper. One of the innkeepers made shoes, one of the bakers kept a shop, and one of the carriers was a general dealer – in other words he bought and sold practically anything! By 1939 the population had declined, and the list of trades had been reduced to one cobbler, one carrier, three innkeepers, three general shopkeepers stocking branded goods (one kept the Post Office, another baked and sold bread), and a basket-maker on the point of retirement. On the other hand, a sawmill had been successfully established – again a development akin in some respects to the story of George Sturt's family business, and with some interesting implications for the future.

What, then, was the general situation of country trade at the beginning of the Second World War? Among those serving agriculture, the blacksmith, the wheelwright, the saddler, the thatcher, and a few others were still in fair demand, although the tendency was for one man to serve a territory that supported several of his predecessors. In some cases the practice was to visit the principal villages one or two days every week or fortnight, after the manner of the solicitor or doctor. In others it was possible to run several trades together, as already described. In a few instances new

* Penguin Books.

prospects were being opened up. The blacksmith, for example, was beginning to adapt himself to the needs of power farming, and with the assistance of the Rural Industries Bureau was learning new methods of welding and installing up-to-date plant. As for the woodland and osier crafts, here was still some activity, although failure to replant was seriously reducing the sources of supply. Hurdle-making, basket-making, and the manufacture of scythe sneads and handles of all kinds, cribs, besoms, ladders, and many other products of coppice and plantation all continued in many parts of the countryside. Nevertheless, the trade was vulnerable to mass production methods and substitute materials. In building, tradition was also in decline, but this was, perhaps, the most prosperous of all rural industrial employments. Bricklayers, carpenters, plumbers, plasterers – although all were losing their country flavour – still had plenty of work, for the demand for houses and repairs was not lacking. In pottery it was a mixed report. The manufacture of land drains, flowerpots, and of some sorts of brick was still quite prosperous, but tremendous competition existed for the cheaper article. A few traditional earthenware potteries survived in Dorset, Devon, and elsewhere, making commercial and ornamental ware, but these were exceptional since, for some time past, the trade had virtually been monopolized by large-scale industry in Staffordshire. Only the 'studio' potters – such well-known men as Bernard Leach, Michael Cardew, and others, who had founded their own small country businesses – seemed to be developing along new lines; but their output was small and, of necessity, expensive. Finally, all over the countryside, there was still in aggregate a quantity of survivals for which there seemed only a limited future – windmills, watermills, ropewalks, charcoal kilns, and some cottage industries. In a few cases strenuous efforts were being made at preservation. Some, such as stone quarries and slate mines, had unique access to raw materials that were still needed. Others, like the watercrafts (boat-building, crab- and lobster-pot making, net and cordage manufacture, etc.) maintained a traditional market that might well continue. But the future of country trade does not lie with the exceptions. It lies to some extent with the progressive craftsman who can make use of machinery; but to a far larger extent with the small up-to-date village factory capable of absorbing most of the labour surplus to the requirements of the land. However, this is a contentious subject and will be discussed further in Part Three.

Wheelwright

3

The Administrative Element

IN a democratic country, government depends to a large extent upon the manner in which it is delegated, and upon the quality of the local councils and their members to whom executive power is entrusted. In England the village has always been not only the smallest unit of administration but also, for centuries, the only real one in the everyday life of the countryman. Historically the origins of village government might well be discovered in the primitive assemblies of the prehistoric tribes, which successively invaded and colonized the English countryside at large during the three thousand years preceding the Claudian conquest of A.D. 43. In fact, so little is known about primitive affairs that, for practical purposes, most historians make the manor their starting-point. Now it is considered that the manor had its beginnings in England among the Anglo-Saxon and the Scandinavian communities, and it may even have existed as early as the sixth century. In Norman times it provided the framework of rural civilization, by regulating the practice of agriculture and by administering the civil affairs of the community that lived within its boundaries. Terminology is confusing, but for the sake of accuracy it must be emphasized that 'manor' was by no means synonymous with either 'village' or 'parish'. Originally 'manor' was a seigneurial term denoting a piece of property or estate, while 'village', 'vill', or 'township' were administrative terms denoting units of civil government, and 'parish' was an ecclesiastical term denoting a district served by a priest. In point of fact, as time passed the three terms drew closer together both in meaning and in function. Thus a manor often did contain one village and its associated hamlets, which in turn were circumscribed by the parish boundary. So, for the purposes of this chapter, no fine distinction will be drawn between the three except where necessity demands it.

In early years the Manor Court was the instrument of village government, and its scope has already been described. The lord presided and, in theory at any rate, the jury of villagers decided. Early in the fourteenth century the court was divided into Court Baron and Court Leet. Court Baron dealt with all matters relating to the custom of the manor, while Court Leet was principally concerned with petty justice. Both courts were supervised by the lord's deputy, the steward, who was generally a lawyer, and judgements were executed by the bailiff. It was not long, however, before the judicial functions of the Court Leet were absorbed by the Court of Quarter Sessions, and by the higher courts. Court Baron continued in effective existence at least until the middle of the sixteenth century, while both courts have survived until recent times as anachronisms.

Some time in the sixteenth century, or even earlier, the church began to supplant the manor as the arbiter of village affairs. The decline of feudalism and the onset of capitalist enterprise were the dual cause. For ecclesiastical purposes the parish was administered by the vestry-meeting or vestry, which was originally an assembly of all the parishioners, presided over, *ex officio*, by the priest. Soon it became the practice at the annual meeting held after Easter, called the 'open vestry', to appoint an executive committee of one or perhaps two dozen members (usually the leading figures of the village) to conduct the day-to-day business of the parish. The open vestry also selected the parochial officers, of whom the most important were the churchwardens. In 1601 the Poor Law finally placed all responsibility for village affairs upon the shoulders of the vestry, and in doing so merely confirmed a process that had been working itself out over a number of years. Henceforward all those manorial officials who survived became the servants of the vestry, in particular the constable, the waywarden (or surveyor of the highways), and the fieldmaster or reeve who attended to the conduct of open field farming. Besides this, the Act charged the churchwardens with the care of the poor, and appointed new officials called overseers to assist them. As 1601 is a climacteric in the history of the village, it is necessary to investigate the duties of these officials, and their subsequent development.

CHURCHWARDENS

Each parish was provided with two churchwardens (usually men, occasionally women), known respectively as the People's Warden and the Rector's or Vicar's Warden, chosen, as the names imply, by the parishioners and the priest. The office was an annual one and unpaid, but expenses were fairly generously conceded and a yearly dinner was awarded on release. Although, in many respects, the churchwardens were the most important of all the village officials, no property or other qualification was required for either post. On the other hand, a property test was sometimes employed in order to combat the tendency to evade duty when obligations became onerous, and in this way householders were sometimes elected by 'houserow' or in rotation. Plainly church maintenance was a primary duty, and this will be described in the next chapter, but while at first civil commitments did not amount to very much (e.g. making payments for the destruction of vermin), the

EXTRACT FROM THE
CHURCHWARDENS' ACCOUNTS FOR TRULL (SOMERSET),*
1577

Item paid unto Xpoffer[1] Pullman for a planke & the
    settyng thereof uppon the churche dowre   vj^d

,,   ,,   for oyle agaynst alhallondaye[2] for the belles   ij^d

,,   ,,   at the laste vicitacion at Taunton   vj^s vj^d

,,   ,,   unto Mr Anthonye our curat towards his
    chargis to cary the regestor bocke to Mel-
    verton   vj^d

,,   ,,   for oyle for the bells & candells to gyve lyght
    to the ryngers that ronge for the reioysynge
    of the quene maiests raigne whiche I praye
    God longe to contynew &c.   iij^d

,,   ,,   for a breckfast for the ryngers at Nycholas
    Heryngs being in number xv men   ij^s x^d

,,   ,,   unto Nycholas Heryng for his fee to see the
    bellis in order   iiij^s

,,   ,,   John Bull & for iiij steripes[3] to make fast a
    pee[4] uppon the fowrthe bell & for a plat[5] for
    to sett uppon the wheale & nayles   x^d

,,   for the churche house rent   ij^s vj^d

    1. Christopher.
    2. All Saints Day.
    3. Stirrups (iron rings or bands).
    4. A weight.
    5. 'Plat. Anything flat or horizontal, as a piece of timber so laid in
building, etc.' (Halliwell's *Dictionary of Archaic and Provincial
Words*).

* See footnote on next page.

EXTRACT FROM THE
OVERSEERS' ACCOUNTS FOR BANWELL (SOMERSET),*
1722–3

	li	s	d
Paid for stockings for Jno: Norman	00	1	0
,, for makeing the Rates for the window tax	00	3	0
,, Ann Helliar 11 months pay at 4s per month	02	4	0
,, Ann Helliar for looking after John Norman 11 months	00	16	6
,, for a Coffing for Ann Helliar	00	8	0
,, for wooll[1] for her	00	1	6
,, for bread & cheeze at her burial	00	3	6
,, for bear & syder & tobacco when she was stretcht out, Coffinged & at her burial	0	8	9
Ringing ye bell & makeing her grave	0	3	6
Paid Charles Fisher 6 weeks pay	00	6	0
,, Charles Fisher from ye 11th of August to ye 21th of Aprill it being 9 months at 4s per month	1	16	0
,, Ann Rogers 10 weeks at 2s	01	0	0
,, Eliz Ney one months pay at 12s per month & 5 weeks pay at 2s per week	01	2	0
,, Mary Androse 2 months pay at 4s per month	00	8	0

1. Acts 18 & 19 Car. II, c. 4 (1666), 30 Car. II, c. 3 (1678), and 32 Car. II, c. 1 (1680), concerning burials in woollen.

* I am indebted to Mr I. P. Collis, Somerset County Archivist, for these two extracts from Churchwardens' and Overseers' Accounts; the former by kind permission of the Rev. C. W. Trevelyan, M.A. These documents are contained in collections of records deposited by the Incumbents and Councils of the parishes concerned, for preservation in the Somerset Record Office, and for the use of the student. V.B.-C.

accounts that were kept are an important source of information about country life in the past; especially where the subject matter was not strictly adhered to, and marginal notes were inserted, often of a scandalous or comic nature. When the overseers were instituted, both they and the church-wardens were charged with the administration of the Poor Law. For this reason, and because joint records were often kept, it is difficult to decide where their respective duties began or ended. The necessary distinction can rarely have been strictly observed, and in some cases the offices were amalgamated. Since this was an irregular practice, Poor Law business, which formed the bulk of local government work between 1601 and 1834, will here be regarded as the province of the overseer.

OVERSEERS

The overseer was first known in 1572 as a collector of alms for the poor. In 1601 his position as a regular parish official was confirmed, and two, three, or four overseers were chosen by the vestry for annual appointment by the Justices of the Peace. The office was unpaid and carried a vague and unspecified property qualification. The multifarious duties can be summarized as follows: care of the sick and 'impotent' poor by providing hospitals or out-relief; finding work and supplying raw material for manufacture by the unemployed; dealing summarily, with the aid of the constable, with 'sturdy vagabonds'; apprenticing poor children; levying parish rates to meet all the expenses incurred. Between 1601 and 1834 a multitude of Acts were passed in an attempt to solve the worsening problems of poverty through the medium of the parish; and for a hundred and fifty years parochial officials were able, more or less, to discharge their tasks. Certainly the immediate effect of the

1601 Act was beneficial – vagrancy was brought under control, and the worst forms of destitution were relieved, although the obligation to provide employment was quickly dropped. Soon Houses of Correction, which had been known before 1600, were adopted on the basis of one per county, places which accommodated, apparently indiscriminately, beggars, thieves, 'lewd women and bastards', and parents who had abandoned their children. In 1662 the Act of Settlement was passed which, in effect, converted the parish into a prison for paupers. This question of settlement was not new: overseers already had the power to remove the recalcitrant and the impotent to their place of origin. After 1662, however, no man was permitted to settle anywhere other than his own birthplace, unless he could prove substantial means of support; a principle so inhuman that it was constantly evaded by overseer and pauper alike. In consequence a series of new Acts had to be passed (in 1685, 1691, 1696–7, 1722–3) to render the scheme workable. The original means test was based on the occupation of property with a minimum annual value of £10. Later this was extended to residence in the parish for forty days after due notice to the official or for a year without notice, to the payment of the parish rate, to serving a parochial office, or to being bound in apprenticeship to a parishioner. Harvest was always an exception, but even then a stranger had always to carry a certificate from his native parish agreeing to take him back, and at all times poor persons travelling outside their home had to carry certificates of a similar type, in case they became chargeable on the rates. This slight concession was offset by a shameful regulation that compelled all paupers to carry a badge (the letter P) on their right shoulders, non-compliance being severely punished.

In spite of restrictions and severities the system never

really worked. Settlement cases were always coming up – indeed they formed a major part of Poor Law business – and were fair game for the lawyers. In the first place correspondence was necessary in order to establish a pauper's place of settlement; then, if no court action was necessary, followed the actual removal by the parish constable, who accompanied the pauper (and, perhaps, his family) to the parish of birth, or at least as far as the county boundary. If the new parish proved obstinate the pauper was returned, and this might happen seven or eight times until the court was resorted to, or one side gave in. In such a case, and there were many, the total bill probably exceeded by far the sum that would have been necessary to maintain the pauper in the first instance. Indeed by 1815 the annual cost of Poor Law litigation had risen to over £250,000, and, besides this, the unemployment which was behind all poverty was being aggravated, not alleviated by the system.

By the end of the eighteenth century new methods in farming and wholesale enclosure of land were beginning to destroy the old pattern of country life. In village as well as in town the population was rising fast. These changes produced new wealth and new poverty on a scale unknown before, and vastly added to the burden of parish government. If the rigours of the Poor Law were in any way lessened, that was due as much to the inability of the overseers to cope with the work as to deliberate humanitarianism on the part of authority. Nevertheless the public conscience was at last being aroused and several measures came into force that eased the worst miseries. For instance, in 1781–2 Gilbert's Act was passed with the object of reforming workhouses. Now, workhouses had been in existence since the end of the seventeenth century, and they were the indirect outcome of that part of the 1601 Act which enjoined overseers to find work for the unemployed. In 1722 parishes had been permitted either to contract with an individual to lodge and employ the poor or to combine with other parishes in the provision of a common workhouse. It can be seen, therefore, that any system whereby the overseer could order a pauper to the workhouse instead of awarding him or his family out-relief was open to abuse. For that reason village workhouses were generally insanitary and overcrowded places, but they were popular with the authorities in that they pressed less heavily upon the rates than other forms of relief. Gilbert's Act, though only adoptive, humanized workhouse conditions by introducing paid guardians and by awarding powers of supervision to the Justices of the Peace. But even this well-meant reform came to be ill used, especially in the apprenticeship of pauper or bastard children. Until 1757 indentures had always been required, but after that date any legally stamped document would serve, even an entry in the parish books. Thus village apprenticeship often became a fiction, and children were disposed of at random to any farmer or housewife who wanted a drudge. In aggregate, there were a large number of Poor Law reforms, but all attempts at improvement were constantly being vitiated by the sheer weight of poverty and distress.

By the first decade of the nineteenth century it had become impossible to cater for all the workless in the workhouse, and so a new policy had to be adopted. The embodiment of this new policy was the Speenhamland system whereby, as noted in Part One, out-relief was liberally given in the form of supplements to wages. In each case, the sum paid was related both to the current price of bread and to the size of a man's family. Thus a large family became a wise investment and, with wages in the region of a shilling a day, it paid almost as well to be kept by the parish as to be earning a living. The repercussions of Speenhamland were disastrous – early and prolific marriages, and illegitimacy are obvious examples. At the same time no effort was made to house the growing population; some landlords, in fact, were actually pulling down cottages and destroying smallholdings, in order to reduce their liability for rates. In the past, women with illegitimate children had been sent to a House of Correction, but after 1750 illegitimacy became so widespread that bastard children were supported by the parish as a matter of course, although every effort was made to trace a father and make him responsible for a child's upkeep. Forced marriages were also quite common, an overseer or churchwarden giving away the bride or acting as best man. Another repercussion of Speenhamland was the development of systems for the hire of pauper labour. In several parishes so many able-bodied labourers were forced upon the rates that the overseers were ready to offer any kind of inducement to the farmers to take the men on. One expedient was known as the 'Roundsman System', which dated from the days of Gilbert's Act and had several variations. An overseer would send a labourer *round* from one employer to another, working a week or two for each. A low wage was agreed and the poor rate added in the normal way. Alternatively the employer contracted with the parish for the man's labour, and the parish paid the man. Or again, a labourer might be put up for auction, and the highest bidder would secure his services. Another method was the 'Labour-Rate System', whereby the employer was excused the payment of rates if he guaranteed to employ a certain number of pauper labourers. Lastly there was the 'Gang System', by which the overseers contracted direct for farm work with men organized in gangs.

The first thirty years of the nineteenth century were a period of unmitigated misery for the poor, who attributed all their troubles to the overseers, the most hated men in the village. While conceding the undoubted callousness that existed, it must be said that the parish was trying to operate a system that was practically unworkable. And so long as the overseers were volunteers and members of the village, there was a degree of humanity in everything that was done. But when paid or 'standing' officers were permitted after 1815 to deal with the volume of work, then the element of humanity disappeared. However, the end was now not far off. By 1817 poor rates were costing the country £10,000,000 annually, a rise of £8,000,000 in thirty years, and protests were being heard on every side. A public inquiry was ordered, and Parliament passed a few minor vestry reforms, but the public was far from satisfied. Finally the Act of 1834 removed the administration of the Poor Law from the parish altogether. Instead parishes were combined into 'unions', to which workhouses were allotted – a term commonly applied to the workhouses themselves. These 'unions' were administered by locally elected Guardians under the centralized control of the Poor Law Commissioners in London. Out-relief was severely restricted and the workhouse test reintroduced. The village overseer was not abolished, as might have been expected, but survived as late as 1927, chiefly as the assessor of parish rates.

CONSTABLE

The parish constable was a volunteer appointed every year by the Justices of the Peace, and until 1842 no property qualification was required. He was the direct descendant of the manorial headborough, tithingman, or tuttiman. He is known to have existed in the thirteenth century, and his powers were both wide and summary. Principally, of course, he was responsible for the maintenance of law and order in the parish, and he had the power to arrest any offender and put him in the village lock-up. Then there was a whole range of routine police duties that had to be performed, e.g. the checking of alehouse licences, or the forwarding of hues and cries (proclamations for the arrest of criminals). The stocks, whipping-post, and ducking-stool were all in his charge, and he had to administer beatings to vagrants and others who were liable to punishment. Military matters were also in his province. In medieval days he must maintain the archery butts and take good care of the parish armour, often stored in a room over the church porch. He was responsible for delivering levied men to the muster, and for arranging their pay; later he had similar duties in respect of the Militia. Besides this there was a mass of work, impossible to classify or even identify as solely his responsibility. A typical list might include the presentment (sworn report) of non-churchgoers, the custody of the parish bull, convening public meetings, rendering assistance at a wreck (in a coastal parish), supervision of the beacon (if any), return of jury lists, paying poor travellers, collecting the county rate, etc. In fact, the variety and quantity of obligations was so confusing that any normal householder, serving his turn, never attempted more than a few of them, nor would he look for any trouble in the matter of offenders. Nevertheless as Poor Law administration increased, extra duties fell to the lot of the parish constable. A frequent task was the removal of settlement cases (unless the parish had already agreed the work with a contractor), or of accompanying vagrants and prostitutes to the House of Correction. Like the other officers, the constable submitted annual accounts which were met by a special rate, and where extant these can still be seen together with the other village registers and documents in the parish chest. By 1856, the constable had ceased to exist as a parish officer. Instead he had become a paid member of the County Police Force.

WAYWARDEN OR SURVEYOR OF THE HIGHWAYS

This was a voluntary annual office with no specific qualification. It was of feudal origin, when the repair of the parish roads was an obligation fulfilled in the normal way by the custom of the manor. As feudalism declined, however, so the state of the roads deteriorated, and travelling became almost impossible. In 1555 the Highway Act reiterated the liability of the parish to maintain its own roads, and this decision held good for some three hundred years. It required every parishioner of substance to contribute to roadwork a horse and cart and two men for four days in the year; others were to work themselves. Later the period was extended to six days. The waywarden in charge had at one time been appointed by the parish, but after 1773 his nomination had to go forward for approval to the Justices of the Peace. Three times a year he had to report the condition of his roads to Highway Sessions. His expenses were met by a highway rate imposed by the parish, although by the eighteenth century so little money was being spent that highway items were often included in the poor rate. It naturally followed that the state of the roads was extremely bad, and this was one of the contributory causes of the Turnpike Trusts, established to improve main roads and make those who used them subscribe towards their upkeep by means of tolls. Parish labour remained obligatory, however, and in the early nineteenth century paupers were often put to this sort of work, if no other form of employment could be found. In 1835 a new Highway Act made an end of compulsory work and substituted highway rates for minor roads, but the main roads were still left to the

Turnpikes, now hard hit by the loss of parish labour. Finally, as a result of railway competition the Turnpikes disappeared, and by the Act of 1862 main road repair was thrown back upon the parish in the form of higher highway rates. For this purpose parishes were grouped together into Highway Districts, waywardens were abolished, and the rates heavily subsidized. Finally all rural highway matters were transferred to the County and Rural District Councils at the end of the century.

* * *

In describing the wide scope of village government, the impression may have been given that no effective supervision was exercised over parochial affairs. This is not the case, for although a great deal of latitude did exist, the village was by no means free to govern itself in any way it pleased, and in most civil matters the vestry was subordinate to Quarter Sessions and its officers, the Justices of the Peace.

JUSTICES OF THE PEACE

In his book *English Social History*,* Professor G. M. Trevelyan writes this:

The institution of Justices of the Peace, local gentry appointed by the Crown to govern the neighbourhood in the King's name, was a move away from inherited feudal jurisdictions. But it was also a renewal of the movement towards bureaucratic royal centralization: it recognized and used local connections and influence for the King's purposes, a compromise significant of the future development of English society, as distinct from that of other lands.

Indeed history, which gives rise to this judgement, con-

* Longmans.

firms not only the dual nature of the Justices as provincial and royal officers, but also their indispensability to parish government. Their origin was an ancient one, dating from 1195 when certain Knights were 'assigned to enforce the taking of the oath to keep the King's Peace'. Later 'they received judicial powers' and in 1362 they came to be known as 'Justices of the Peace, in which year was ordained they should hold Quarterly Sessions'.* One of their chief duties was to assess wages locally, but by Elizabethan times their powers had been considerably extended. As servants of the Privy Council they had to enforce Government policy in the provinces, and in this way they controlled not only wages but prices, especially of bread. In addition they dispensed summary justice and supervised the administration of the Poor Laws. In the latter case, although content and ready to leave details to the parish, they always retained certain specific duties. For instance, in settlement and vagrancy they were responsible for the examination of cases and for the issue of certificates, removal orders, and the like. As for relief or workhouse matters, they could and frequently did override (or confirm) the decisions of the overseers. Similarly the waywarden and the constable were both directly responsible for the discharge of their duties to the Justices, who also exercised control over all parish appointments, except that of the churchwardens. In the Commonwealth they even supplanted the parson and were empowered to solemnize marriages, although this was not frequently done. By Hanoverian times, Justices of the Peace were still nominally responsible to the Crown, although in fact they owed their own appointments to the Lord Lieutenant of the county, who in turn was guided in his selection by the leading property

*Quoted from *The Care of County Muniments*, by G. Herbert Fowler (County Councils Association).

owners. This was their period of unpopularity. Trevelyan writes later in the same book:

In the middle year of the [eighteenth] Century, Fielding, Smollett and other observers of the injustices of life, bitterly satirized the irresponsible power of the J.P.s and its frequent mis-use in acts of tyranny and favouritism. There was a corrupt type of J.P. known as 'trading justices', men of a lower order of society who got themselves made magistrates in order to turn their position to financial profit. But generally speaking the Justices who did most of the work in rural districts were substantial squires, too rich to be corrupt or mean, proud to do hard public work for no pay, anxious to stand well with their neighbours, but often ignorant and prejudiced without meaning to be unjust, and far too much a law unto themselves.

This appraisal of their qualities accounts for such contrasting behaviour as the well-meant though calamitous Speenhamland decisions and the callous and repressive enforcement of the law in respect of petty offences in the first part of the nineteenth century. When the care of the poor was lost by the parish in 1834 and the vestry began to decline in executive importance, so too did the Justices suffer a gradual eclipse. Eventually most of their administrative powers were forfeited to the County Councils, so that today J.P.s are primarily magistrates, retaining a few powers in connexion with licensing and other matters.

SHERIFF

Another office-holder of significance to the village, although at a greater remove than the Justice of the Peace, was the Sheriff. Originally this was a Saxon title, Shire-reeve, and referred to the officer who administered the shire on behalf of the King. After the Norman Conquest the office was considerably strengthened, and the Sheriff—usually a baron—

became the chief source of royal authority in the provinces. With the decline of feudalism, however, the Sheriff gradually diminished in importance, and nowadays his position is largely ornamental. Even so the 'High Sheriff' still retains a few duties, and these include attendance on the judges at Assizes, responsibility for the execution of writs and sentence of death, preparation of the panel of jurors for Assizes, safe custody of prisoners, etc. He also acts as returning officer at Parliamentary elections.

* * *

We now come to the last phase in parish history. For nearly three hundred years the vestry was the master of the village, but under the Local Government Act of 1894 it was finally deprived of all its civil powers, and thereupon it reverted to its original status as a unit of church government. In its place was set up the Parish Council, a purely civil body, and also the Rural District Council, which with the County Council (created in 1888) completed the structure of rural administration. That is still the position today. The village is governed, directly and indirectly, by all three Councils, and although their respective powers and relationships have been extended and amended by further Local Government Acts, it is not proposed to examine the details too closely. Instead a brief survey of the way in which each separate Council impinges upon the village must suffice.

THE COUNTY COUNCIL

For the purposes of representation on the County Council several neighbouring parishes are amalgamated into a Division, which returns one member to County or Shire Hall. A candidate must normally reside or own property in the Division, suffer no legal disabilities, and fulfil the normal requirements of age, nationality, and sponsorship. As member he will serve probably on at least two committees (possibly on many more), according to his abilities and the amount of time he can devote to the work. If an active man he will hold regular meetings in all the villages belonging to the Division and keep in touch with outstanding parish problems, but particularly with those which are the special responsibility of the County Council. These are, in the main, Education (the village primary school, the secondary school, adult education, and all the recreational services which the County Education Committee renders to the village), Planning, Highways, Smallholdings, Police, Health (e.g. District Nurse, Ambulance, etc.), Fire, Welfare, Children, and Records. The County Council is also the electoral authority.

THE RURAL DISTRICT COUNCIL

In this case representation varies considerably in different parts of the country, but usually a large village is allotted two or even three members, while a small village may have to share its member with its neighbours. In general candidates have to qualify in the same manner as for the County Council. Obviously the scope of the Rural District Council is narrower than that of the County Council; on the other hand it is more intimately concerned with village life. Its most important function, perhaps, is Housing – the building of working-class cottages and the licensing of private contracts. The Council is also actively concerned with water, sewerage, refuse collection, certain health matters, and with the collection of rates. Contact between the village and the Rural District Council is maintained both by the member and by correspondence between the District Council and the Parish Council, to which the former should act

as guide and support in practically every matter the Parish
Council cares to raise.

THE PARISH COUNCIL

The foundation of all village government is the Parish
Meeting, an assembly of all the parish electors, who must
meet together at least once a year. To possess a Parish
Council, the population must either exceed 300 (in which
case a Council is compulsory) or be between 200 and 300
(in which case a Council is permissible). If a parish has a
population of under 200 and wishes to set up a Parish
Council, then authority has to be obtained from the County
Council. The number of parish councillors varies from five
to fifteen, according to the size of the village, and qualifications for candidature are normal, but include residence in
the parish (or within three miles of it) or ownership of
property. Elections are held every three years, voting by
ballot has now been made compulsory, and at the first meeting of the Council (and thereafter annually) a Chairman is
elected, either from among the Councillors present or from
outside the Council altogether. Meetings are usually held
at the primary school or at the village hall, and must not be
less than four a year, including the annual Parish Meeting.
In fact, a number of active Councils meet far oftener —
monthly or bi-monthly at least. The Clerk may be one of
the Councillors, but in that case he may receive no re-
muneration. It is usual, therefore, to make an outside
appointment and pay a small salary of from £5 to £20 per
annum, although a few exceptionally large villages are able
to afford a much higher figure. The Clerk's duties are to
keep the minutes, records, and accounts, and summon
Council meetings, which he attends in the role of adviser
on all matters pertaining to powers and procedure. It is

therefore essential he acquaint himself, as fully as he can, with the scope of parish government; other than this, however, he should in no way interfere with the discussions and decisions of the Council. A Treasurer is also required, a post often filled by one of the local bank managers. In all other respects, the business of parish government is conducted in the normal manner, either in camera or, if the Council agrees, in public.

Curiously enough, the effective powers of the Parish Council are not easy to define, for much of the ground available is covered by other organizations. For instance, there are four Acts which may be adopted by the Council – the Lighting and Watching Act, 1833, the Burial Acts, 1852 to 1906, the Public Improvements Act, 1860, and the Public Libraries Acts, 1892 to 1919. Of these only the first two have wide application. Many Councils light their own village streets, while burial powers are also occasionally used to provide a cemetery. Libraries, on the other hand, are now a County matter, and public improvements such as public walks, shelters, playgrounds, etc., are generally obtained in other ways. Similarly a Parish Council is empowered to provide and maintain a village hall or a playing field, but traditionally this is the work of voluntary organizations, who are likely, however, to call upon the Parish Council for assistance.

Nevertheless there are two matters in which the Council is directly interested – Allotments and Rights of Way. If there is a demand for allotments, the Parish Council may borrow money to buy and manage the land, or delegate the management to a responsible body, such as an Allotment Association. Sufficient rent must be charged, however, to make the undertaking solvent. Rights of way are essentially a parish responsibility, and the Council still has voluntary powers to maintain footpaths, footbridges, stiles, and gates, and this is particularly useful in cases of emergency. Where permanent improvements are required it can now call upon the County Council, as the Highway Authority, to carry out the work. If obstructions are put up by land-owners or farmers, or if footpaths get into a bad state, then it is the bounden duty of the Parish Council to take effective action, and call in higher authority if necessary. In general most farmers will see to it that all their stiles and gates are kept in reasonable order, for it is in their own interests to do so, and it saves the Parish Council and the ratepayers much trouble and expense besides. In the past this question was much aggravated by the lack of official maps, but now under the provisions of the National Parks and Access to the Countryside Act, 1949, active steps are being taken to survey all rights of way, and draw up a map and schedule showing the accepted public ways in every parish. This should solve some long-standing difficulties.

Finally the Parish Council is able wholly to administer or to share in the administration of local charities, to appoint managers to the village school, and to exercise a long list of miscellaneous powers which cannot be specified here. In all these matters, however, the field of action is bounded by considerations of finance. A Parish Council may spend up to the limit of a 4d. rate in any one year, or if the Parish Meeting agrees up to 8d., exclusive of expenditure under the Adoptive Acts. Beyond this, approval must be obtained from the Ministry of Local Government. The product of a 1d. rate varies between £2 and £12 in the majority of villages with less than 600 inhabitants. In larger villages the yield is generally higher. In any case the total is never very high, and by the time the Clerk's salary and a number of statutory charges have been paid there is little left to work with. It is possible, however, to bypass the Parish Council altogether, and petition the Rural District Council to appoint in its place a Parochial Committee, consisting, normally, of members of both Councils. The Rural District Council can then delegate all its powers, except finance, as they affect the area concerned, to the new organization. Where this has been done, the results have been quite satisfactory and parish government has benefited, but the procedure is not widely known and, on the whole, has been but rarely used.

There is, however, another more successful aspect of the work of the Parish Council — that of acting as an intermediary in matters of purely village concern. If, for instance, main water is needed, or a bus service, if new houses are wanted or a public telephone box, if a by-road needs making up — in these and a hundred kindred matters the Parish Council can be of great assistance. First it should investigate all such requests and then forward them, *on behalf of the community*, to the appropriate quarter — whether Rural District or County Council, Post Office or elsewhere. Conversely the Council can serve higher authorities by keeping the village informed of official business which bears on local life.

In this way the Parish Council has already done much to justify its half-century of existence and to offset its lack of executive authority.

4

The Religious Element
Church : Chapel : School

CHURCH

T H E part played by religion in the history of the village is so great and yet so diffuse that it is not possible to determine its precise extent. Even the origins of church organization are difficult to fix, but it is at least known that by the later years of the Roman occupation Christianity had been officially established in Britain. It disappeared, however, with the Anglo-Saxon invasions, and returned only during the sixth and seventh centuries by way of Celtic missionaries from Ireland and Scotland and of Continental missionaries from Italy. The two missions soon clashed, superficially over the method for deciding the date of Easter, but fundamentally over the question of supremacy; and at the famous Synod of Whitby held in A.D. 663 under the presidency of Oswiu, King of Northumbria, the dispute was finally settled in favour of Rome. Thereafter events moved apace. Under Theodore of Tarsus, Archbishop of Canterbury from A.D. 668 to 690, the church was organized into dioceses, and a rough unity obtained at a time when the temporal power was still being contested by the three major kingdoms of Northumbria, Mercia, and Wessex. Subsequent history is not within the scope of this book, but at least it can be said that by the year 700 the English Church existed as a national institution; and that upon the foundations laid then rose the structure, first of the medieval, then of the Reformed Church, and indeed of the Anglican communion as it is today.

E.V.—6

THE PARISH AND THE PRIEST

The origin of the country parish is obscure, but it is usually attributed to two parallel schemes of organization dating from the Anglo-Saxon period. One was occasioned by the necessity for decentralization within the diocese, which prompted the bishop to dispatch certain of his officers to take charge of rural areas. The other was the appointment by local magnates (with the approval of the Diocesan) of purely village priests to serve newly built churches on manorial estates. There is no doubt that this was the commoner practice, and the incumbent, although instituted by the bishop, looked to the lord for his support. His cure, also, was generally limited to the inhabitants of the manor, and in many cases the ecclesiastical and the civil boundaries were identical. Thus were established at an early date both private patronage and the parson's freehold, elements of the English church that have survived to this day. In the former case, an advowson (or right of presentation to a benefice) was so closely connected with landownership that it became, in effect, a piece of property itself. This was good in so far as it ensured continuity of tradition and patriarchal interest in a village; but it was bad where commerce in advowsons was encouraged, and in those numerous cases where family livings were *automatically* filled by relations of the patron. The fact, too, that a parson, once appointed, could not be shifted against his will, unless he had committed a crime, was altogether a mixed blessing; for while it strengthened liberty of conscience, it also made an unworthy man safe against authority.

At all events, the priest was early established as the spiritual leader of the village community. He also carried out a number of extraneous duties associated with his vocation. He was the registrar for baptisms, marriages, and burials, he provided references as to character for any person requiring a licence (e.g. for an alehouse) or for a candidate for public office. Until the close of the sixteenth century he was directly charged with the problems of the poor, and with all matters concerned with their welfare. Even after the Poor Law of 1601 he continued, as chairman of the vestry, titular head of all village administration, although in fact the work was mostly carried out by parish officials under the authority of the Justices of the Peace. In addition he was a teacher, and in early days he was often the only man in the village who could read and write.

TITHE

As a reward for his services the priest was accorded a number of privileges. He could refuse any of the civil or manorial offices, all military duty, and membership of a jury; and right up to the sixteenth century he was virtually exempt from civil jurisdiction. His precise status was not easy to define. In feudal times the priest fitted into the manorial scheme like one of the tenants. In many respects he was at the same social level as the villein, but his house and the land that he cultivated were free of rent in terms of money, produce, or service, other than the exercise of his calling. Gradually his standing improved, but while continuing for centuries to farm his own holding or his glebe, he was by no means financially independent, and increasingly relied upon the community for support in the form of tithe. Now this was originally a voluntary offering, consisting of one-tenth of the annual yield of stock and crops, or of the products of personal industry, and had been devoted either to the relief of the poor, or to the general expenses of the Church. From about the tenth century onwards it became a compulsory tax, and was levied for the particular benefit of the priest. As an institution, tithe was never popular, and village people constantly had to be exhorted, cajoled, or threatened in order to secure payment. It was further complicated by division into 'great' and 'small' — 'great' being calculated in corn, hay, and wool, 'small' in everything else. In early days, when land was granted or willed by pious persons to cathedral chapters, monasteries, or other ecclesiastical bodies, it was the custom for the latter to appropriate the great or rectorial tithe, and leave the small to the priest or vicar (deputy) whom it appointed to the living. At the Dissolution, most monastic possessions, including advowsons and rectorial rights, passed into the hands of laymen; as a result, complexities and abuses increased fourfold. Some countrymen (the Quakers, for instance) refused on religious grounds to pay at all, but the problem of definition was far more serious, and endless cases were fought to decide what was titheable and what was not. An extreme but entertaining example* was the case of the vicar who claimed payment upon the *wild* ducks taken in an East Anglian decoy, but losing his case (because they *were* wild), then claimed a tenth of the eggs laid by the *tame* ducks used in the same decoy. All this bickering did harm to the relations of villager and priest. For the one it was a hindrance to honesty and good farming, for the other it was often onerous and disagreeable. Nevertheless so long as subsistence agriculture was carried on in the open fields and commons, tithe collection in kind was just feasible. The produce was stored in the tithe barn (often a fine piece of architecture), and the parson himself remained a practical agriculturist right up to the nineteenth century.

By this time, however, although many private settlements were already in force, the demand for the general

* Quoted from *Foundations of Agricultural Economics*, by J. A. Venn (C.U.P.).

commutation of tithe had become very insistent. The county reports of the Board of Agriculture, for example, issued between 1790 and 1815, all condemned open field agriculture and tithing in kind as being the chief obstacles to high farming. Nevertheless opposition by the clergy remained, largely because the commutation value was estimated as likely to be less than the value in kind, and so attempts to alter the custom were for the time being frustrated. Even so, in many cases of enclosure, it was possible to extinguish tithe by allotting land in lieu to the titheholder, who was also excused the legal and the fencing liabilities incurred by the allotment. Finally, as noted elsewhere, according to the Tithe Act of 1836, arrangements were made to replace tithing in kind with a rent charge, based on the price of corn averaged over seven years. In general this Act held good for nearly a century, until new legislation in 1918, 1925, and 1936 standardized payments and introduced a system of redemption. As a result tithe is now being gradually extinguished, and the Church is being compensated with Treasury stock. The parson's stipend has therefore been divorced from any direct dependence on the land, and in the light of history this must be considered an advantage. At the same time, the gradual disappearance of tithe and the fact that an incumbent no longer farms his own glebe have almost severed the Church's practical connexion with agriculture, and that is of doubtful benefit to the country clergyman.

ADMINISTRATION

The control of the village church was, primarily, the concern of the parish priest; but not later than the fourteenth century he was receiving the assistance of two lay officials, the churchwardens, and of a council of villagers, the

vestry; and these have already been mentioned in connexion with civil affairs. In ecclesiastical matters the
churchwardens were charged with the care of the church:
and this included the maintenance of fabric and furniture,
upkeep of the graveyard, and custody of the parish stock.
Before the Reformation the latter consisted of a quantity of
cash, goods, and cattle, which belonged to and were traded
in for the benefit of the church. After the Reformation, the
stock was converted into a reserve of raw materials, such

FIG. 24. — *Graveboard*

as wood, wool, thread, and the like, intended for the employment of the industrious poor. Likewise the churchwardens had charge of all arrangements for the performance
of miracle plays, for the brewing of church ales, and for the
observance of all the traditional festivals and entertainments
that were ultimately abolished by the Puritans. During
Divine Service it was their duty to keep order, and in this
they were assisted by sidesmen and by the parish clerk, an
official chiefly deputed to lead the congregation in the
singing. At all times they had to keep accounts, and here
were many items of interest. Probably the first annual entry

referred to expenses incurred at the visitation of the archdeacon or of the bishop, by whom the churchwardens had to be confirmed in office, and to whom 'presentments' were made twice yearly; that meant reports on misconduct by parishioners or even by the priest. In early days there were many items relating to candles for special Masses, rushes for the floor, boughs and flowers for holy days; and even after the Reformation the wardens continued to purchase the bread and the wine and any utensils required for church services. Other recurrent charges included repairs to the bells and the clock, and certain decorations to the interior; but in this matter the rector had to see to the structural repair of the chancel, while the nave remained the responsibility of the parishioners. Although technically the seating (if any) was free, in fact the allocation of pews devolved upon the churchwardens, and by the eighteenth century private pews were a feature in most churches. Lastly, during any vacancy, whether by death or for any other reason, the churchwardens were held personally responsible for the care of the church and all its property. When, by the Local Government Act of 1894, the Parish Council replaced the vestry as the unit of civil administration in the village, much of the importance attached to the office of churchwarden disappeared. This was taken a stage further in 1921 when many of the remaining duties were transferred to the Parochial Church Council, an elected body of churchgoers who, under the chairmanship of the incumbent, now see to all matters connected with the upkeep of the church and graveyard, and in many instances with the parson's stipend as well. The vestry, too, has largely been displaced, and now has an almost nominal existence; but it is still held once a year, after Easter, and may be attended by any ratepayer in the parish for the election of church officers and to receive the accounts of church charities.

At one time the village church depended for its income upon the levying of a special 'church rate'. With the increase of Nonconformity this practice declined and, after much agitation, was abolished in 1868. Nowadays revenue is obtained in the main by collections, subscriptions, and other voluntary offerings – a state of affairs reminiscent of the early days of parish history.

THE PARISH CHEST AND ITS CONTENTS

From the first the church was the repository of many of the village treasures. There were several reasons for this. For one thing, the church itself was often the centre of community life; it was not only a place of worship, but also a village hall, and a point of assembly. Up to the Reformation a number of parish churches undoubtedly owned chests for the safe keeping of valuables and documents, and these were usually placed, not in the sacristy (which was a rarity in the medieval church) but in some convenient position in the body of the building. Then, in 1538, Thomas Cromwell, minister to Henry VIII, publicly commanded every parish to acquire a 'sure coffer' with two locks (keys to be kept by parson and churchwardens respectively), and to keep therein the newly instituted parish registers or official records of all baptisms, marriages, and burials. Later in the century an alms-box had to be provided, and as often as not the two purposes were combined and a single parish chest was installed. These early chests were of the most primitive kind, mere hollowed-out trunks of trees, of great weight and with very small storage space. Subsequently the construction was improved and rectangular boxes were made of oak or elm on the coffin principle, with iron bands and locks; alternatively 'Armada' chests of solid iron were imported from the

Continent. As the years passed, parish chests followed the current fashions in furniture, and there are some very elegant examples in walnut and mahogany dating from the eighteenth century. Eventually, when Poor Law business had imposed a mass of papers on every parish, large iron boxes became popular – but these were capacious rather than beautiful. Nowadays many churches or parsonages are provided with modern safes for the preservation of records and of church plate; while the county archives and the local bank are available for rare documents and valuables. Although much good material has, in the past, been deliberately or carelessly destroyed, the parish chest is still an excellent source of historical information. And in any country church one would expect to find at least some of the following:

REGISTERS

These date from Thomas Cromwell's order of 1538, and at first entries were often made on loose sheets of paper. But in 1597 Convocation ordered that these older entries be transcribed into parchment books, 'but especially since the first year of her Majesty's reign' (1558); and these are usually the earliest registers extant. During the Commonwealth, parishes suffered much through the dispossession of episcopalian incumbents by ministers of Presbyterian persuasion, and for a time the church was deprived altogether of the right to solemnize matrimony. Weddings had to take place before magistrates, while the registers were placed in the care of a new official, 'the Parish Register' (*sic*), who was often the Parish Clerk. In 1666 and 1678 legislation was passed which enforced the burial of corpses in wool, and there are many entries to this effect, and certificates. By Lord Hardwicke's Marriage Act of 1755 the whole system of entry was standardized and reformed. Banns were introduced, and both parties had to sign an official printed form inserted in a bound book, but even this law was not universally obeyed. After 1837 civil registration supplemented church records, and nowadays all entries in church marriage registers have to be in duplicate, one copy being sent to the civil registrar. Finally, it is common knowledge that parish registers are an occasional source of village history, through the practice of making marginal notes. Many of these are entertaining, a few are truly historic, but the majority are merely trivial. They include references to such matters as the Civil War, disputes between the minister and his officials, perambulations of the parish boundary, the weakness of midwives for liquor, farming operations, medical recipes, and many other things.

ACCOUNT BOOKS

There were two principal sets of accounts – the churchwardens' and the overseers'. Strictly speaking the former dealt with church expenditure and incidental civil items, while the latter was concerned with all aspects of poor relief. In fact both sets often overlapped, and no definite distinction can be drawn between the two. Occasionally, also, separate accounts were kept by the constable and, more rarely, by the waywarden or surveyor of the highways, but normally the expenditure incurred by these two officers was incorporated in the two principal books. Lastly, there may be found the accounts and proceedings of village charities. Few of these have an origin earlier than the Elizabethan period, for most of the medieval foundations disappeared at the Dissolution of the monasteries. Even since then a large number of charitable benefactions and endowments have been lost either through carelessness or through the misappropriation of funds. In many instances the churchwardens devoted the charitable moneys to the relief of the rates. The Charity Commissioners, who now regulate such matters, have done much to retrieve ancient endowments, but if in modern times it requires constant watchfulness to keep a charity intact, how much more difficult must it have been to do the same in the past. Most village charities belonged to one or more of four main categories – the supply of fuel, of food, or of clothing for the poor, and the education of the young; but that was not all. For instance,* money was left for bell-ringing, for setting young men up in business, for providing cows and commons for the landless, or for such frivolities as distributing forty dozen buns by throwing them off the church tower, or even for an annual wrestling match.

MISCELLANEOUS

Other records to be found in the parish chest might include Vestry Minutes and Agreements, all the Poor Law paraphernalia (viz. Removal Orders, Examinations, Settlement Certificates, Apprenticeship Indentures, Vagrant Passes, Bastardy Bonds, etc.), Visitation Records, Tithe Maps and Apportionments, Enclosure Awards, Briefs (collections in church for good causes), Glebe Terriers (inventories of church property in the parish), and many other documents that, strictly speaking, had no right to be there at all; for example wills, court rolls, census returns, railway and canal plans, etc. Nevertheless, the fact that such things have frequently been discovered in the parish chest supports the claim that the church was for centuries the true centre of the village, and it is there the historian must first look if the life of the countryside is to be placed on record.

* See *The Parish Chest*, by W. E. Tate (Cambridge University Press), from which these examples are taken.

THE CHURCH ITSELF

It has been explained that the initial purpose of the parish church was to serve the community both as a public building and as a place of worship. The site, then, was of first importance, and was chosen from considerations both of

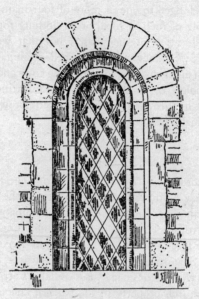

FIG. 25. — '*Norman*' *Window*

prestige and of practical necessity. Many a church tower, for instance, has acted as a landmark to travellers riding across country, or as a lookout against cattle raiders, or as a refuge from flood and fire. As a rule, the building itself was divided into two. The east end, or chancel, was the only part specifically regarded as sacred, and it was usually secluded behind a rood-screen. The remainder of the building, or nave, when not required for Divine Service, was free for public business and entertainment.

As to architecture, no Roman churches have survived in England, and most Saxon buildings have been so altered that few distinctive features remain. The Normans, however, initiated a vigorous phase of church architecture that can be discerned today in the thick walls, in the mouldings

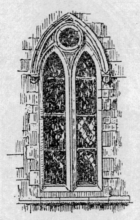

FIG. 26

above round-headed doorways and arches, and in the stone carvings of numerous village churches. This style anticipated the greater glories of medieval architecture, and the four hundred years that separated the reigns of Richard I and Henry VIII yielded a wealth of fine stone churches, representing every stage in the development of the so-called Gothic style of building. This term comprehends certain basic characteristics. One was the advance in structural technique, which rendered the massive Norman walling unnecessary. It was replaced by a much lighter construction whereby the outward thrust of the roof was counteracted at selected points by external buttresses. This made possible higher, thinner walls, and a much larger area of fenestration. Another characteristic was the pointed arch and the developments that it produced, notably in the

FIG. 27

windows whose changing patterns and traceries indicate successive stages within the Gothic period. The examples shown in Figs. 26–29 (re-drawn from Edmund Sharpe's *Decorated Windows*) illustrate the four principal stages: Early English (early thirteenth century), Geometrical (late thirteenth century), Decorated (early fourteenth century), and Perpendicular (late fourteenth and fifteenth

centuries). Improved lighting encouraged interior decoration, and the walls of many village churches were covered
with splendid paintings depicting scenes from the Bible, or
the Day of Judgement. Not only did this add dignity and

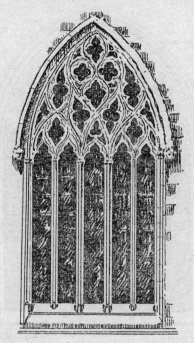

FIG. 28

the perpetual shock of colour, but also it was the means of
teaching unlettered peasants the rudiments of the Christian
Faith. Stained glass windows served a similar purpose.

As the sixteenth century advanced, so gradually the
Gothic style lost its identity. The Middle Ages – that era
distinguished by the monastery, the manor, and the gild –

were beginning to disappear. In church building the impetus of piety diminished, and the secular influences of the Renaissance, no less powerful in their way, began to take charge. Subsequently, in the seventeenth and eighteenth

FIG. 29

centuries, architecture discovered its chief glories in houses and public buildings. That did not mean that from time to time fresh parish churches were not erected about the countryside, or that many existing churches were not remodelled, in the interior at any rate. But by now most villages had acquired a permanent place of worship that was medieval both in origin and in external appearance. In fact, it was not until the nineteenth century that a new architectural force, the Gothic revival, swept over the countryside. As to that, opinion is still divided. Numbers of fine old churches (many probably in a state of ruin) were unimaginatively restored, and Gothic features manufactured where none existed before, in the belief that this was the only true ecclesiastical style. Unfortunately Victorian Gothic is, as a general rule, a poor substitute for the original, both in appearance and in the atmosphere it engenders. Each age makes its own mark, and in terms of architecture the Victorians failed because through imitation they tried to resurrect the past; and that is virtually an impossibility. Had they absorbed the medieval tradition, and not aped it, they might have made a valuable contribution to the architecture of the village.

Finally, reference must be made to the conduct of worship and to the furniture associated with the church. As noted, the interior of the building was divided into two by the screen. This was a substantial construction, provided with a loft for the particular use of the musicians. Choirs were an exception in the medieval church; instead, one or two practised performers, called chanters, led the congregation in the singing, supported in many instances by a small band of string and wind instruments or by an organ. After the Reformation, the screen fell into disuse, and in many churches galleries were built at the west end, which then became the musical centre of the building. The whole tendency of the Reformation was to concentrate attention upon the pulpit at the expense of the altar, and it was not until the nineteenth century that this process was reversed. The implications of this change were widely felt. For instance, in the Middle Ages there was a rich diversity of altar hangings and frontals that varied according to the calendar — white for the first four weeks of Lent, red for Passiontide, and blue, green, or gold for Saints' Days and Festivals. Much of this was abandoned under reforming influence, and only recently has it been tentatively revived and systematized. With vestments and clerical dress the story is much the same. The Puritans were for the abolition of all Roman fashions, but at first their arguments were too violent for the majority of churchmen, who continued to wear the cassock and the surplice for all services; no doubt some retained the older Mass vestments as well. During the Puritan ascendancy, however, the black Geneva gown and bands became customary, and this seems to have remained the normal dress of the village parson for several hundred years. Finally, thanks to the Oxford Movement, pre-Reformation practice was partially resumed, and nowadays the parson generally wears a black or grey suit and clerical collar outside the church, and surplice, stole, and hood, or some vestment, for the conduct of Divine Service.

At one time the pulpit grew to immense proportions, and rose two or more storeys, the upper regions for the preacher, the lower for the parish clerk. The congregation, too, was more comfortably accommodated. In early days all had stood, except the old and infirm, who were given special seats along the wall ('the weakest go to the wall'). However, as the pulpit was promoted and sermons lengthened, so pews were introduced, the wealthy renting their own. It was not long before 'family pews' became a byword — some were spacious chambers, as tall and as roomy as horse-boxes, and equipped with a fireplace. Such material comfort led inevitably to decadence, and the simplification of church seating became one of the major reforms of the Victorians.

THE COUNTRY PARSON IN HISTORY

Integrity and a strong personality are the chief assets in the management of village affairs, as indeed they must be in any profession that deals with human beings. And throughout English history there has never been any lack of village parsons who possessed these virtues. Some, however, have distinguished themselves in other ways as well – in learning, politics, science, and in the practice of the arts. It would not be difficult to make an impressive list of names, especially in the medieval period, when minor orders were easily come by, and when most settlements outside London were no larger than large modern villages. And so, to illustrate rather than justify the point, the following may be regarded as a striking but by no means a comprehensive list.

We begin with Richard Hooker, Elizabethan divine and rector of Boscombe in Wiltshire, where he completed his *Laws of Ecclesiastical Polity*. In the same county we find George Herbert, the poet, author of many delightful hymns and of a critical study of the parson and his office, entitled *A Priest to the Temple; or, The Country Parson, his Character and Rule of Holy Life*. A more robust character was Robert Herrick, rector of Dean Prior in Devon, and a lyric poet of genius, who delighted in the half-pagan festivals of the countryside. He was expelled during the Interregnum, not so much for his royalism as for the fact that he approved of the traditional gaieties of the church. It is quite true, of course, that religious behaviour had become lax, but zeal carried the reformers too far. Not only did they put an end to a multitude of ancient religious customs that had long sustained the English countryman, but they wantonly destroyed church furniture and ornament and stifled the artistic impulses of religion. Not all the Puritans were extreme. Richard Baxter, rector of Kidderminster, was an acknowledged example of moderation and good sense; another was Thomas Traherne, the mystic, of Credenhill in Herefordshire. By the early eighteenth century the fires of fanaticism had died down, and the country parson was liberated to think and act as he pleased, even to the extent of abandoning his cure altogether. Such was Gilbert White who, although a fine character and much loved in his native Selborne, saw nothing wrong in drawing the revenues of a distant living in Northamptonshire, of which he was the official but absent incumbent. George Crabbe, the East Anglian poet, was another notable absentee, and so was Laurence Sterne, a good writer but a most unsatisfactory country parson. By contrast, the Lakeland teacher Robert Walker spoke with the true voice of charity and conscience; and James Woodforde, the diarist, no less charitable but more concerned with the welfare of his stomach. As might be expected, the nineteenth century introduced new and vigorous types of rural clergymen. There was the evangelical, inspired by Wesley and Wilberforce. There was the ritualist such as John Keble, rector of Hursley. There was the radical such as Charles Kingsley at Eversley, and Canon Girdlestone at Halberton, the champion of the agricultural labourers. Again there were scholars and writers – William Barnes of Winterbourne Came, R. S. Hawker of Morwenstow, Sabine Baring Gould of Lew Trenchard, Francis Kilvert of Clyro, and J. C. Atkinson of Danby in Cleveland, author of *Forty Years in a Moorland Parish*. These men have all left behind an invaluable record of the old civilization of the countryside before it entirely disappeared. In contrast, there was Froude, the Exmoor parson, a bully and a rascal; or the amiable and popular Jack Russell, one of the keenest hunting men of his day, who nevertheless squandered a large part of his wife's portion on his favourite sport.

As yet, the twentieth century is too young for judgement, but it must be said that the parson has declined in the estimation of the village. Perhaps it is because his prerogatives of property and education have lost their validity, and because so many of the services rendered by the church have now been appropriated by other institutions. Moreover, it is a situation in which all the denominations find themselves — not only the Anglican Communion. Yet there is still scope for the man with a true vocation; unlike Sydney Smith who wrote in 1838: 'I have no relish for the country; it is a kind of healthy grave.' But Smith did himself an injustice. He was a remarkable man, and an exceptionally good parson, in an exceptionally bad time.

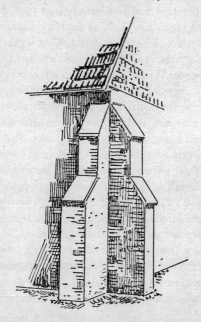

FIG. 30. — *Buttress*

CHAPEL

The origins of Nonconformity in the countryside date from
the sixteenth century, and are ascribed to those ministers
and their followers who desired an absolute reformation of
the English Church. Their theory was that* 'nothing
should be ordered which could not be found in the Bible:
kneeling, for instance, is not ordered there: bishops are only
mentioned casually, without any command that they should
continue: many of the commonest ceremonies of the
Church cannot claim to have the authority of the Bible
behind them'. As a matter of history, the break-away from
the Established Church began in direct consequence of the
Acts of Supremacy and Uniformity in 1559. The former
proclaimed Queen Elizabeth as Supreme Governor of the
English Church. The latter restored the Prayer Book of
1552, at any rate in substance, and inflicted penalties for
non-observance. Within a few years, when it became clear
that the Queen was taking her stand upon the enforcement
of these Acts, the Puritans (the absolute reformers) were
compelled to make their choice. Some 'conformed' and
retained their identity as Low Churchmen, that is, Angli-
cans with Puritanical leanings. Others also conformed but
continued their efforts at reform, and pressed for Presbyterianism, which sought to abolish the episcopal hierarchy
and place the government of the Church in the hands of
ministers and of elders elected by the congregation. These
Presbyterians agitated for a number of years, and in 1643
they gained a temporary ascendancy; but at the Restoration Presbyterianism was officially disowned and the
episcopal system restored. Finally, there remained those
Puritans who consistently rejected the Elizabethan Settle-

* Quoted from *Christianity in England*, by C. A. Alington (Oxford
University Press).

ment, and who were rigorously persecuted in consequence. Known generically at first as 'Separatists', they gradually assumed sectarian identity as Independents or Congregationalists, from principles expounded, in the main, by Robert Browne. Later, as the seventeenth century proceeded, new leaders and new sects arose – the Quakers, the Baptists, and other smaller bodies, some of which have disappeared.

The triumph of Oliver Cromwell (whose army was largely officered by Independents) was the triumph of Puritanism, and under the Commonwealth*

'the Christian religion, as contained in the Scriptures' was recognized as the national religion; all persons 'professing faith in God by Jesus Christ' were to have 'freedom and protection in their ministry and worship so long as they did not disturb the public peace and endeavour to promote Popery or Prelacy'.

This appeared to offer complete liberty of conscience and worship, and in fact a multitude of separate sects sprang to life, although by no means all were tolerated. Also a large number of clergy who had served the old Established Church were rudely deprived of their livings and replaced by 'intruding' Puritan ministers. In 1660 there was a religious as well as a social and political Restoration, and a fierce reaction set in against all forms of Puritanism within and without the Established Church. A series of Acts penalizing all those who refused to conform deprived some two thousand Puritan ministers of their livings, forbade the practice and teaching of Nonconformity, and denied Government or municipal employment to all who held Nonconformist beliefs. Several thousands were arrested, and many died in prison or were transported. There were also many – especially in the countryside – who were

* Quoted from *A Brief History of English Congregationalism*, by Albert Peel (Independent Press).

befriended by Anglican sympathizers and continued to meet in secret.

A typical example was that of Peter Ince, quoted by the Rev. Alfred Antrobus in his *History of the Wilts and East Somerset Congregational Union.**

Peter Ince was dispossessed of his living at Donhead St Mary two years before the Great Ejection, and was imprisoned at Dorchester for a considerable time. On his release, he found employment as a shepherd on the estate of Mr Groves, local Member of Parliament, and was apparently unrecognized. His wife falling ill, Mr Groves sent a message to the vicar of the parish asking him to call, and received the reply that the vicar was just setting out with the hounds, but would come over on his return. Observing the annoyance of the master, one of the servants said to him, 'Our shepherd can pray very well, as we have heard him praying in the fields.' The shepherd was sent for, and prayed with such helpfulness that Mr Groves perceived he was no ordinary farmworker. Learning that he was Peter Ince, in charge of the nearby church some years before, he made him his chaplain, and the services he conducted at Ferne House were the beginning of the Birdbush Congregational Church.

Of all the sects, there is little doubt that the Quakers suffered the worst persecutions, and excited the strongest feelings of admiration for their endurance and steadfast behaviour. In spite of this, there were certain areas (especially the North of England) where they established strong links with the countryside, and where in due course the tight little Quaker colonies succeeded in exerting an important influence upon the life and trade of the neighbourhood. Meanwhile, the campaign against Nonconformity continued, and it was not until the Toleration Act of 1689 that the worst disabilities were removed. Immediately a remarkable recovery took place, for by 1700 at least a

* Independent Press.

thousand meeting-houses had been erected by the principal Nonconformist persuasions, and many private rooms were licensed in addition. But the impetus was not long maintained and during the first part of the eighteenth century there was a period of religious quiescence, a reaction no doubt from the many years of controversy and strife. For the Established Church it was the age of rationalism, and of an economic security that corrupted the country clergy. To Nonconformity it brought a temporary decline in influence and, possibly, in numbers. Within a few years, however, the evangelical revival of the Wesleys and George Whitefield swept through the countryside. Initially this was not a separatist movement. John Wesley remained a member of the Anglican Church all his life, and it was not until after his death in 1791 that his followers adopted independence. The Methodists owed their success partly to the fact that they appealed to the emotions in an age surfeited with reason, and partly to the practice of open-air preaching – on the village green or in the fields – to that large mass of the population which had been neglected by the church. Their example was soon followed, and evangelicals (those concerned with the saving of souls as opposed to the solving of the intellectual problems of religion) were active within the Established Church as well as in other branches of Nonconformity.

Throughout the entire course of the nineteenth century the numbers of rural chapels steadily increased. Most villages and hamlets acquired one or more meeting-places of Nonconformist denomination; and even where membership was sparse the preacher would be certain of a keen attendance. The impact of the chapel upon village life was very great. For one thing it seriously weakened the established order of rural society. Squire and parson and the principal farmers had ruled as they pleased for several hundred years. They had a strong grip upon the sources of employment, while the means of spiritual independence – literacy, for example – were still largely in their hands. Thus it was that the chapel became a social and a political refuge, as well as a religious one, that strengthened and sheltered the lower ranks of agricultural society – the labourer, the craftsman, the smallholder and small farmer. By its agency*

innumerable small groups came into existence, governing their own affairs, having their own unpaid teachers and preachers and paying their own way. In the chapels the labourers learned self-respect, self-government, self-reliance and organization; here men learned to speak, to read, to write, to lead their fellows.

Often the chapel building was bare and ugly; where money was short, materials were cheap and coarse, and style had to follow suit. It represented very well the temper of chapel folk, who had few reserves and little disposition to compromise. One of the most vivid accounts of the chapel in village life is Richard Jefferies' tremendous though wayward essay *The Country Sunday*. Jefferies was no partisan of religion; in institutional form he often abused it, but here he writes with the intensity of the microscope.

Of the chapel itself, he says:

This great building, plain beyond plainness, stood beside a fir copse, from which in the summer morning there floated an exquisite fragrance of pine. If all the angles of the architects could have been put together, nothing could have been designed more utterly opposite to the graceful curve of the fir tree than this red-bricked crass building. Bethel Chapel combined everything that could be imagined contrary to the spirit of nature, which undulates.

* Quoted from *Sharpen the Sickle*, by Reg. Groves (Porcupine Press).

Of the creed and the people, he says:

A grimly real religion, as concrete and as much a fact as a stone wall; a sort of horse's faith going along the furrow unquestioning. The doctrine at Bethel was the one saving doctrine, and there they went ... the men in their black coats and high hats, big fellows that did not look ungainly till they dressed themselves up; women as red as turkey-cocks, panting and puffing; crowds of children making the road odorous with the smell of pomade; the boys with their hair too long behind; the girls with vile white stockings, all out of drawing, and without a touch that could be construed into a national costume – the cheap shoddy shop in the country lane. All with an expression of Sunday goodness: 'Today we are good, we are going to chapel, and we mean to stay till the very last word. We have got our wives and families with us, and woe be to any of them if they dare to look for a bird's nest. This is business....' Old women – wonder 'tis how they live on nothing a day – still manage to keep a decent black dress and come to chapel with a penny in their pockets in spite of their age and infirmities. The nearest innkeeper, himself a most godly man, has work enough to do to receive the horses and traps and pony carriages and stow them away before service begins, when he will stride from the stable to the pew. Then begins the hollow and flute-like modulation of a pitch-pipe within the great building. One of the members of the congregation who is a musician is setting the ears of the people to the tune of the hymn that is about to be given forth. The verse is read, and then rises the full swell of hundreds of voices; and while they sing let us think what a strange thing the old pitch-pipe – no organ, no harmonium – what a strange thing the whole scene is, with its Cromwellian air in the midst of the modern fields.

He then describes what happens after the service is over:

All those who have come from a distance have brought with them their dinner in a black bag or basket, and quietly settle themselves down to take their dinner in the chapel. This practice is not confined to pilgrims who have walked a long way; very many of those who live the other side of the village shut up their cottages, bring their provisions, and spend the whole day at their devotions. Now the old woman spends her Sunday penny. At the back of the chapel there is a large room where a person is employed to boil the kettle and supply cups of tea at a halfpenny each. Here the old lady makes herself very comfortable, and waits till the service begins again. Halfpenny a cup would not, of course, pay the cost of the materials, but these are found by some earnest member of the body, some farmer or tradesman's wife, who feels it a good deed to solace the weary worshippers. There is something in this primitive hospitality, in this eating their dinners in the temple, and general communion of humanity, which to a philosopher seems very admirable.

Of the minister he paints a cheerful but unfamiliar picture; unfamiliar, considering the strong views that most chapel folk still hold about temperance:

There is no man so feasted as the chapel pastor. His tall and yet rotund body and his broad red face might easily be mistaken for the outward man of a sturdy farmer, and he likes his pipe and glass. He dines every Sunday, and at least once a week besides, at the house of one of his stoutest upholders. It is said that at such a dinner, after a large plateful of black currant pudding, finding there was still some juice left, he lifted the plate to his mouth and carefully licked it all round; the hostess hastened to offer a spoon but he declined, thinking that was much the best way to gather up the essence of the fruit. So simple were his manners, he needed no spoon; and, indeed, if we look back, the apostles managed without forks, and put their fingers in the dish.... Very frequently another minister, sometimes two or three, come in at the same time, and take the same dinner, and afterwards form a genial circle with cognac and tobacco, when the room speedily becomes full of smoke and the bottle of brandy soon disappears. In these family parties there is not the least approach to over-conviviality; it is merely the custom, no one thinks anything of a glass and a pipe; it is perfectly innocent; it is not a local thing, but common and understood. The consumption of brandy and tobacco and the good things of dinner, tea, and supper (for the party generally sit out the three meals), must in a month cost the host a good deal of money, but all things are cheerfully borne for the good of the church.

That was the canvas of the nineteenth-century rural chapel, but Jefferies adds one illuminating touch which shows that the village, in spite of sectarian dissension, was still a close community:

If any one fell ill he had to be content with the workhouse doctor; if they required anything else they must go to the clergy-man and get a letter of introduction or some kind of certificate for a London hospital, or any infirmary to which he happened to sub-scribe. The chapellers made no bones about utilizing the clergy-man in this way; they considered it their right; as he was the parish clergyman, it was his place to supply them with such cer-tificates.

This illustrates perhaps best of all the difference between chapel minister and parson. In the eyes of the village the latter was, like the constable, a permanent official who con-trolled their destinies, although to a less extent than for-merly. The minister, on the other hand, was one of themselves; not permanent at all, for he held office by per-mission – their permission. Of course, since Jefferies wrote, events have greatly altered the stratification of the village, and they have swept away most of the tensions and planned inequalities that produced the religious and social rivalries of the past. In addition, there is now a strong movement for union between the various Dissenting bodies, and signs of a far closer co-operation than in the past between Non-conformity in general and the Established Church. The importance of this is made plain by the small attendances at practically any village church or chapel. Doctrinal differences fade into insignificance when compared to the general apathy towards institutional religion.

SCHOOL

The school forms part of the religious element of the village, in that all education originated with the Church. Very little is known about medieval education, but it is likely that the parish priest gave religious instruction to the village children and that he held classes in some corner of the parish church. If a pupil showed aptitude he might enter an endowed grammar school; otherwise the village child stayed at home and at an early age was put to work on the land or apprenticed to a trade. The Reformation put an end to many religious foundations and, in theory at any rate, to the priest's monopoly in teaching, although both Edward VI and Elizabeth ordered the clergy to instruct their parishioners in reading and writing. Much, however, was left to the individual, and most country parsons did little beyond teach the catechism, although even this was sometimes delegated to the parish clerk. Of course, there were notable exceptions. Bishop Ken, for example, was active in founding parish schools, while the Society for Promoting Christian Knowledge, established in 1698, was largely responsible for the Parochial Charity Schools that flourished for about a century. The Nonconformists, too, were active in this direction.

Education in the countryside, however, was not widely provided until the second half of the eighteenth century, when the work was being undertaken by private schools conducted for profit, and by philanthropic schools. The first category was very large. It comprised dame schools, that is, classes of young children up to seven years old supervised by an old woman in her cottage – the crude equivalent of the crèche and the infant class; also evening schools of the type attended by William Cobbett's father when he was earning twopence a day as a ploughboy. At some schools teaching had to be combined with business, a master might be a shopkeeper, or a mistress might take in laundry; such schools were often attended by the poorest children, who would not otherwise have received any education at all. Again, there were the endowed schools and a number of Dissenting academies, while in many country houses the squire retained a private chaplain as the family tutor. The philanthropic school, on the other hand, had a somewhat different purpose. Its chief aim was to inculcate morality and lessen the miseries of pauperism, which by 1800 had reached monumental proportions. Poverty was not understood in economic terms at all, it was generally attributed to laziness; thus the curriculum in this type of school was invariably based upon the Bible and, in an Anglican institution, upon the catechism. One of the earliest philanthropic foundations was the Sunday School, a movement started by Robert Raikes, a Gloucester journalist, in the year 1780. These schools were undenominational but gave Bible instruction and were strongly supported by churchmen of all creeds; and by many others, if for no better reason than that they permitted the children to go to work on weekdays. Child labour was, of course, nothing new, but the Industrial Revolution had brought the whole subject into prominence, and many so-called 'schools of industry' were set up in workhouses and attached to factories where the children were taught the three Rs.

By 1800 the philanthropic movement was in full swing, and within a few years it was strengthened by the foundation of two societies, which between them were to provide the majority of voluntary elementary schools in England. These were *The National Society*** set up in 1811 on strictly Anglican principles, and *The British Society*† in 1814 which was undenominational but attracted a strong Nonconformist backing. Both National and British schools were organized on monitorial‡ lines and catered for pupils between the ages of seven and ten. At first they were free, but when money ran short they began charging small fees, and from 1833 they received some financial help from the Government. By 1870 it was calculated that about one and a half million children were attending these schools, or about half the available school population. But it was recognized that the time had come for a truly national system of education that would provide for every child of school age. The State, on the other hand, was seriously hindered by the religious difficulty, one which even now has not been satisfactorily solved. The step taken in 1870 was to pass an Act that allowed for a dual system of control. According to this

---

* The National Society for Promoting the Education of the Poor in the Principles of the Established Church throughout England and Wales.

† The British and Foreign School Society.

‡ 'Setting pupils to teach pupils.'

the Voluntary Schools were permitted to continue, and State* Elementary Schools provided to fill the gaps; these were organized under School Boards (thus 'Board Schools') and supported by the rates. In 1902 School Boards were abolished and the control of rural elementary education handed over to the County Councils. However, the system of local management was retained, and the Voluntary Schools continued as before. In addition the County Councils were given powers to establish secondary schools to which pupils from any elementary school (county or voluntary) could gain admission by scholarship at the age of eleven. In 1918 the Fisher Act finally fixed the school-leaving age at fourteen (without exception) and provided a more advanced and practical curriculum for the older pupils. This tendency was further developed, after 1926, as a consequence of the Hadow report, and many elementary schools were reorganized into senior or central (i.e. centrally placed) schools for children between the ages of eleven and fourteen, and into infant and junior schools for those between five and eleven. Later the school-leaving age was raised to fifteen, but this provision was annulled at the outbreak of war.

Such was the general background of events before the passing of the 1944 Education Act. But since this Act is, perhaps, representative of the tremendous changes that have occurred as a result of the War, it would be of interest, first of all, to consider pre-War village education. Moreover, while it is true to say that changes and improvements had constantly been taking place ever since 1870, there existed a strong feeling that 1939 marked the end of a well-defined period in educational development, and that a new

---

* This is a term of convenience. In fact such schools have always been administered by local bodies, and not by the central government direct.

Act was required to point the way to the future. Take, for example, the typical school buildings described by H. M. Burton in *The Education of the Countryman**:

Our nineteenth-century village schools may be found beside the duckpond, at windswept crossroads half a mile from the village, in dank hollows, on the edges of wild commons or disused sand-pits, on steep slopes or on the summits of sharp little hills.

Architecturally the schools were not less varied than the sites. The most frequent type was the ecclesiastical. From the outside these schools look like small chapels. They have a steeply Pitched roof, tall lancet windows beginning some five to eight feet from the ground, little Gothic porches and a bell-turret.... Inside, these buildings most often contain one long large room – anything up to 1,500 square feet – and a small additional class-room. The roof is so lofty that one or two blazing coal fires are seldom enough to warm the air in winter until well into the afternoon – but these rooms are usually pleasantly cool in hot weather. The whole picture is by no means unpleasant; it has the mellow and friendly air of a room that has been much lived in, and many a great and lonely man at home or abroad looks back with affection on the homely bustle of his village school.

The walls are often of undressed brick above the level of the children's heads. Below that they may be plastered and distempered or panelled in pitch-pine or deal, stained and varnished a melancholy brown. Sometimes there is a ceiling within sight; sometimes the dim mysterious heights recede far above the children's heads, often with a leaky lantern in the middle; occasionally, also, there are birds' nests.

In most rural areas the old long desk is disappearing, with few to mourn its end. It was, indeed, a sad survival. Often it had no back-rail and the children either 'slumped', and developed round shoulders, or sat back with the desk behind digging painfully into, or just below, their shoulder-blades. Out of the five to seven who shared the desk, only those at the ends could move with comfort or without disturbing all the rest; and the squeaking and banging

* Routledge & Kegan Paul, Ltd.

when all stood up was appalling.... The more modern idea is the dual locker table, with separate chairs, and this seems, for general purposes, the most satisfactory of all. Two or more can be placed together for needlework or some other craft; the tables are comparatively light; and the chairs can be used by adults.

We have seen how thoughtlessness in the choice of site often led to the school being built in places where it was almost impossible to provide a suitable playground; but even where there is space to spare, and level space at that, the country playground is still often a handicap rather than an advantage. Probably about half of them are gravel-surfaced; if the gravel is good these playgrounds are very fair in dry weather; after one storm, or in ordinary wet weather, they are a series of pools and wet stones. If the gravel is inferior they are much worse, and at the best of times gravel is unpleasant to fall on. A very large number, however, are not even gravelled; they are just rough earth, with tree-roots, large stones, ugly ruts and depressions, even rubble and brick-ends freely scattered about.

Across the playground are the closets and the urinals, usually known by the genteel name of 'offices'. For the urban visitor these will hold the biggest shock of all; he will think that nothing could be more vile and primitive for children, and he will recoil in horror when he hears that the teachers must use them too.... But on the whole there is not much cause for complaint. The country child, like his parents, is less sensitive than the town child to unpleasant smells; indeed, after working in a stable yard for an hour or two daily, or cleaning father's boots for years, or watching the cesspool being emptied once or twice, it is doubtful whether the country child notices many things that would make a town child sick. And, apart from aesthetic considerations, the school 'offices' are usually quite harmless; the School Medical Officer sees to that.

As to the teachers, the schoolmaster in the smaller village was already fast disappearing. His life and work are excellently described in *The Dodo** by Vicars Bell, himself

* Faber & Faber, Ltd.

master of the village school at Little Gaddesden in Hertfordshire. Often, say in a two-class school of fifty, the head teacher was a woman, frequently a married woman living with her husband in a tied house next the school. Her salary, which had been systematized by the Burnham Scale, was approximately £100–£150 a year. Her only assistant, another woman, had originally been a pupil-teacher, but on reaching the age of eighteen became a 'supplementary' teacher (vaccination was the only qualification!) at £50–£75 a year. Nevertheless, despite low scales of pay, inadequate equipment and facilities, and many other handicaps, both women worked extremely hard and were respected by the children. Indeed, teaching was but one of many tasks, which included the distribution of milk, the oversight of midday meals, the collection of national savings, arranging for medical and dental inspections, or raising money for the purchase of a wireless set or of sports tackle for the school. The headmistress in particular had a very long day. After school was over, she would spend an hour or two marking exercise books, preparing lessons for the following day, and seeing to a number of administrative matters. After this she might be expected up at the Village Hall to play the piano at a social, or assist in the organization of the Flower Show, or do the accounts of the Clothing and Boot Club; for like her predecessor, the schoolmaster, she was one of the pillars of village life.

As to the curriculum, the situation is well summarized in the following extract from *Country Planning*,* 'a study of rural problems' carried out in 1943 in an area of Oxfordshire by the Agricultural Economics Research Institute, under the direction of Dr C. S. Orwin:

* Oxford University Press.

In the junior schools, after the Infant stage, the main emphasis is on a thorough grounding in reading, writing, and sums, with some history and geography, scripture, music, handwork, and physical training. Along with this training in the tools of education the child begins to learn something about living in a community.

For all those children who stay on at senior schools, either in their own villages or in neighbouring ones, the curriculum is much the same, with the addition of more English subjects and such science as the equipment of the school and the qualifications of the teachers allow, together with gardening, practical subjects, etc. Scripture lessons are given every day.

And on the subject of the transfer of the village child at the age of eleven to a secondary school:

The difference in opportunities which follows success or failure in the entrance examination is fairly obvious. Success opens the door to the fuller, more balanced, much more interesting life of a secondary school, with its trained staff, its 500 children, and every opportunity for specialization in academic and other subjects, and with the way open to universities, professional examinations, and the rest. Failure, at present, dooms the child to the narrow experience of a village school, with a few score of variously aged companions, and one or two masters, or perhaps a mistress, for the rest of his school life. Under the present system, children in towns are better provided for than those in the country because their senior schools are larger, with more children, more staff, and better buildings.

Finally, the School Managers. It is possible that these were all interested and enthusiastic people, of the utmost assistance to both school and Education Authority, but it is unlikely that this was often the case. Only a few were really qualified for the part, even in a strictly limited field of action. Where enthusiasm was shown, it was often far too parochial, but the usual difficulty was to find people willing to be appointed at all, and in many cases they had to be drawn from that faithful oligarchy which sees to all the public work in the countryside.

The impact of the World War of 1939–45 upon rural life and education was as tremendous as it was unexpected. It began with evacuation, when town and country school-children (and their teachers and parents) were forcibly brought together, with some surprising revelations for both parties in hygiene, behaviour, and kindred matters of civilization. It ended with the Education Act, 1944, which revolutionized secondary schooling and largely removed the prospect of village education for the older children. The main provisions and implications of the Act are as follows:

Publicly provided education is now envisaged as a single process subdivided into three parts – primary, secondary, and further – and is virtually made available to all children without restriction and without cost. At the age of eleven every child will proceed to one of three types of secondary school – grammar, technical, or modern. The choice is not based on competitive examinations but on intelligence tests, on reports of work in school, and on general assessment of character and aptitude. School-leaving age is raised to fifteen and will ultimately rise to sixteen. The new primary (formerly junior) schools are to be thoroughly overhauled from the aspect of accommodation and equipment, of the size of classes, of curriculum, and of the number and quality of teachers. The dual system of Church and State is retained, but the managers of the church or 'aided' schools are now liable to bear half the cost of improvements and repairs, and these are of a higher and more expensive standard than in the past. This has already resulted in the transfer to County Education Committees of many church schools.

Much controversy has arisen about the probable effects of all these changes upon the village and the village child.

The critics maintain that by sending country children away to secondary schools at the age of eleven the villages will be emptied more quickly than ever before. The curriculum and urban attractions will between them capture a child's allegiance, while the large numbers involved do not conduce to good education, let alone education with a 'rural bias'. In addition the removal of secondary scholars and the closure of small primary schools will deprive the village of yet another natural leader in the schoolteacher. The protagonists of the Act would reply that many secondary schools are located in country towns; some are in the open countryside. In Cambridgeshire, for example, the secondary school forms part of the Village College, an institution that provides all kinds of cultural services to a rural area of about 10,000 people. It is also claimed that the larger organization of the secondary school provides far better facilities for teaching and an altogether wider curriculum than is possible in the village. As for 'rural bias', perhaps the wisest statement is found in the following extract from *The Land, The People and The Churches*,* a pamphlet issued by the British Council of Churches:

The aim of rural education is not any different from that of true education anywhere. Nowhere should education be directed to forcing children along certain avenues of life and excluding them from others. No rural or agricultural bias in education will keep the country child in the country if his natural ambitions lead him to the town and, conversely, it should be remembered that the finest countryman is not necessarily the man who has lived in the country all his life.

But the means by which this aim is to be pursued varies in town and country. The child has to learn, not only from the printed word, but from all that his senses can perceive in the life around him. For the country child this will be the field, hedgerow, wood,

* Published by S.C.M. Press, Ltd, London.

or copse: birds, flowers, trees, animals; and in the study of the locality his attention will naturally be focussed on people and their work. The country child who lives in a small community, where he knows what every building is for and what every person does as a job and how they all fit together, has a far keener awareness of what community means (though neither he nor his parents would use this word) than the child of the modern city or suburb. What he lacks is the means to grow from this limited to a larger sense of community – but at least he begins at the right end. One of the barriers between him and a full cultural education (other than those which exist within the educational system) is that the country child probably comes from a home which bears marks of generations of struggle with hard poverty. Country parents often have large families and many of them have no time for the graces of life and little understanding of what education is all about unless it is something by which their boy or girl can get a better-paid job. Attempts to keep country children in the country by limiting the range of their education run counter both to the best educational thinking and to the wishes of most parents.

5

The Human Element

F O R some years now it has been the fashion to venerate the English countryman. Physically he is depicted as strong, rugged, deliberate, and capable of long hours of unhurried work. Mentally he is considered an individualist, astute beneath a deceptive exterior, and resentful of all forms of interference; at the same time he is regarded as a kindly, homely person and a good neighbour. In this judgement there is a large element of truth, for in some respects the countryman is self-reliant and co-operative to a greater degree than the townsman. It is true, at any rate, of the individual or of the small group, and is the outcome perhaps of the constant competition with Nature, and of the necessity to turn every resource to account. In larger communal matters the countryman is less developed; nevertheless the village, which is his community, is a complex social unit with a history almost as old as man himself. It is of some interest, then, to inquire into the social manifestations of country life, and to consider anew the various factors that assist in identifying the countryman.

First, is there a distinct type of rural man? Without being drawn into abstruse questions of heredity, it may be generally argued that certain physical and mental peculiarities of the early races that inhabited Britain were transmitted to their successors, and are still recognizable about the country today. Ethnologists point to the shape of the skull and assert that the dominant English 'long head' (width less than four-fifths of length) has been inherited from the Mediterranean immigrants of Neolithic times, and from the Nordics, a term comprising Celts, Anglo-Saxons, and Scandinavians. On the other hand the Beaker folk, and those Gaulish tribes who settled in the south-east during the Iron Age, were all Alpines (emanating from Asia Minor) with 'broad heads' (width four-fifths or more of length). And that it is the fusion of all these stocks, their skull formations, together with other physical features, that has produced the prevailing brown hair and medium stature of the majority of English people today. As to temperament and character, some interesting theories have been advanced — that the talent for leadership and organization derives from the Nordics, artistry from the Mediterraneans, industry from the Alpines — but these are at best conjectural. Similarly, suggestions have been made about the distribution of racial stock, but here again the question must be regarded as problematical. In Cornwall, for instance, and in some remote areas such as the Pennines, the predominantly dark population has been described as a survival of the Neolithic settlements. Also over a wide area in the north and east fair complexions are ascribed to Nordic forebears, while the broad heads found in Lincolnshire and in East Anglia are considered a legacy of the earlier Beaker colonization. Perhaps the wisest conclusion is that advanced by Professor Fleure when he says*

when we speak of race-types in Britain we are not thinking of breeds which have kept separate since they evolved in a far-distant past. We are really thinking of groups of associated characters which are frequently handed in one lot together from one generation to another. They may remain or reappear in after ages to give us evidence of elements which long ago entered into mixture which is continually re-sorting and re-mixing as the generations pass.

* Quoted from *The Races of England and Wales*, by Professor H. J. Fleure (Benn Bros).

To conclude – it is reasonable to assume that, so far as ethnics are concerned, there is no strictly identifiable racial type. On the other hand a sense of separatism has long existed in the countryside, the prime cause being racial or tribal. It was evident from the first in the existence and multiplicity of dialects, originally independent forms of literature and speech, descended from the languages of the early settlers. In broad terms these can be divided into three main types – Northern, Midland, and Southern, roughly corresponding to the former tribal kingdoms of Northumbria, Mercia, and Wessex, but with considerable variations. For example, Northern was common both to the Lowlands of Scotland and to the north of England, while some authorities claim Kentish as a separate main type. Furthermore each of these dialects gave birth to a number of sub-dialects, many of which retained their individuality, often in quite small areas, until comparatively recently. To some people dialect signifies little more than a provincial and possibly an inferior variety of speech. This is, of course, a mistake, for the subject cannot be reduced to terms of what is good or bad. Not only are some of the dialect usages older than those of standard English, but also the word 'dialect' may be variously interpreted. To begin with, Standard English is itself a dialect, or at least the descendant of one, the East Midland, which for various reasons gained an ascendancy over the others. Wyld* attributes it to the fact that it was the dialect of London, and that from the thirteenth century onwards the influence of the capital was becoming paramount, primarily through the diffusion of Parliamentary and legal documents. Later, by the agency of the Court and the Universities, this influence was extended to literature, where it was vastly strengthened by the

---

* Quoted from *The History of Modern Colloquial English*, by H. C. Wyld (Blackwell, Oxford).

appearance of Chaucer, who wrote in East Midland English. By the fifteenth century it was sufficiently established to be adopted by Caxton as the vehicle for printing, and thereafter as a literary medium it was never challenged. Speech, however, suffered a much more gradual change, and even as late as the sixteenth century there was little uniformity among educated people. Sir Walter Raleigh, for instance, is said to have spoken broad Devonshire all his life. Nevertheless, as in literature, the same standardizing influences were at work; and by the seventeenth century, except in remote districts, an educated parlance had been evolved. Subsequently a new set of speech variations gradually appeared. These arose from contact between standard English and the regional dialects, and by the desire of regional speakers to master what had in effect become a class dialect.

However, this was a problem that affected the countryman far less than the townsman, and it was not until the twentieth century, when popular education and new influences such as the cheap Press and the motor-car were hard at work breaking down the barriers of time and space, that regional speech began seriously to decline. In recent years this process has been accelerated, under the pressure of two major wars, by conscription and movements of the population to new centres of industry mainly in the south; also by the wireless and the broadening wave of sophistication. This has already resulted in the virtual extinction of many localized forms of speech, and in a profound modification of the main dialects. It is true that steps were taken some fifty years ago by the English Dialect Society, and by numerous enthusiasts who compiled county glossaries, to preserve the vocabularies and usages of the different districts. Nevertheless print can never tell the whole story, for the essence of dialect is contained in three things — vocabulary, syntax, and sound. And whereas the first two have satisfactorily been accounted for in dialect grammars and dictionaries, the third, by its very nature, has not. Sound, it is true, may be rendered by phonetic symbols, but to the un-instructed these are quite meaningless, and surely they can never quite do justice to that subtle range of accent and intonation which makes the countryman's voice come alive. Again, a recording may possibly preserve a representative range of speech, but a record is so often an indication that the object recorded has had its day, and such is plainly the case with all but the main dialects.

Place names are another subject, closely allied to dialect, which bears upon the question of separatism. It must be said again that this is a broad field of study which requires specialist attention if full justice is to be done. At the same time it is not difficult to see that the quantity and variety of place names offer many striking clues to the origins of settlement and to the nature of those regions which still have a character of their own. Obvious examples may be seen in name components such as *-ton* (Charlton), *-ham* (Bisham), *-stead* (Medstead); or *-by* (Barnby), *-thorpe* (Hatherop), *-thwaite* (Seathwaite) — all signifying a farm or kindred form of habitation, Anglo-Saxon and Scandinavian respectively. Then there are the components implying pos-session or association, as in Wok*ingham*, the home of the sons of Wocc; or the family names such as Sampford Peverel and Langton Matravers given by the Normans to the castles, monasteries, and manors founded after the Con-quest. Again there are the topographical clues — *Combe* (a narrow or enclosed valley), *Ewhurst* (the yew wood); and those relating to land divisions — *Mere* (boundary), *Piddle-trenthide* (the 30-hide holding beside the River Piddle); and a myriad others connected with custom, trade, religion, legend, and practically every form of human activity. To the everyday countryman these historical matters may or may not be familiar. To him the names of villages, of farms and hamlets, and particularly of fields, natural features, and parcels of land, normally convey an altogether different kind of meaning. This may be termed a keen sense of property and local pride, which forms part of his mental background, and affords him a feeling of security and independence. Thus while the disappearance of dialect has done much to loosen the ties of local patriotism, the permanence of place names continues, however slightly, to counteract this tendency.

This restricted sense of place reoccurs, of course, in larger form in certain recognizable regions, for instance in East Anglia, in the south-west peninsula, and in the North Country; and even in smaller districts within these and other regions. In the past regional separatism was strong. It was based upon topographical, tribal, and economic differences which by now have been largely neutralized. The people too have greatly altered, and retain only a small part of their former distinctiveness, notably in a modified dialect, and in a certain traditional attitude to life – the bluntness of the Yorkshireman, or the charming indolence of the Devonian. There are also the relics of a regional culture, now rather selfconsciously fostered by certain educationists and writers, who are waging a tough battle against the increasing centralization of the age.

Nowadays far stronger and far more tangible differences exist between countrymen and townsmen as a whole than as between the populations of the various regions. This is the outcome of history, particularly of the Industrial Revolution, when the townsman was experiencing the spiritual and physical degradations of early industrialism, and when contact with the countryside – always a feature of town life in the past – was virtually being cut off. In the country Nature determines almost the entire pattern of living – health, employment, personal habits and recreations, even the mental attitude. In the town the climate is artificial. Man is in stricter control of his actions simply because he can defy the weather. Thus his routine is regular and planned, his entertainments are largely manufactured, and he is less dependent upon the goodwill of his neighbour for the prosecution of his business. In addition he has many organizational advantages, and considerably more time to develop his intellect if he wishes. In consequence, despite the great increase in his material comforts, and despite the fact that he is in some ways more practical and self-reliant, the countryman puts far less trust than the townsman in the invention and ability of man. He knows his own limitations, and he respects absolutely the natural and elemental forces upon which the whole human cycle of birth, life, and death depends. In this sense he is at heart a fatalist, and it is the key to his individuality.

No less striking is the social aspect of this subject. Throughout history the communal life of the countryside has been characterized by its close connexion with the soil. Long ago country people practised pagan fertility rites, offered sacrifices, danced, and worshipped the elements. Such were the obscure and ancient origins of the Christmas mumming plays and of the folk dances that until recently composed the dramatic repertoire of the village. By the end of its natural life, about fifty years ago, the mumming play had acquired a number of extraneous incidents and characters, although at all times it was a strange mixture of ancient and contemporary history. The three principal figures were St George (or King George, or some such hero as Wellington or Nelson), the Turkish Knight (or Saracen or Beelzebub himself), and the Doctor. The story varied; in essence St George fights the Turk, is killed, and is restored to life by the Doctor. It is in fact an allegory of life, death, and resurrection, designed as a commentary upon the cycle of growth, decay, and regeneration of the seasons.

This is also the basic theme behind the folk dances which Douglas Kennedy in his book *England's Dances** explains in religious terms – 'a form of communication with the unseen forces which control tribal welfare and human survival, which provide food, promote fertility and regulate the weather'. There were two main types of folk dance. The Sword Dance, like the mumming play, was a midwinter celebration with an almost identical plot, mimed by the dancers. In this the Fool or Father is the chief player. After a lengthy preamble he is killed by the rest of the company, who lock their swords around him in make-believe of an execution. Soon after he springs up again, captures the Lady (a hermaphroditic character also called the Man-Woman), and the scene ends joyfully. This dance was confined almost entirely to the North of England, particularly to villages in Yorkshire, Northumberland, and Durham. The other dance, the Morris or young men's dance, was performed in the Spring (usually at Whitsun) and was characteristic of the South, especially of the Cotswolds, although it was also known in Lancashire and Cheshire. Here the dance patterns and movements were more lively as pertaining to the season of the renewal of life. Bells, ribbons, and handkerchiefs were in evidence, and a Bush or Bower was set up for the refreshment of the dancers, who were served by the Green Man, another Spring spirit. Apart from the Sword and the Morris there were many local dances and processions, some of little social significance, others such as the Helston Furry Dance or the Minehead Hobby Horse (half a ship as befitting a seaside community) containing relics of the seasonal themes.

* G. Bell & Sons.

With the advent of Christianity many pagan celebrations were adopted by the Church. Deities became saints, and seasonal rejoicings (such as those held at the summer or winter solstice) were converted into solemn Catholic festivals. That is one reason why the social life of the village centred, in early days, upon the parish church. It was then that the nave, the secular portion of the building, and even the rood-loft were used for every kind of dramatic representation. Among these were the mystery or miracle plays, which were crude religious dramas depicting scenes from the Bible, written with the express purpose of instructing and entertaining the community. In due course the rowdyism that invariably attended these performances caused the authorities to forbid the use of the church building. As a result, from about the fourteenth century onwards, all public amusements were removed to the churchyard outside or to the village green. Here, too, the Maypole was set up, the sideshows and booths, and all the paraphernalia of festival and parish wake.

Soon after the Reformation the miracle plays and many other social manifestations of the Church declined and disappeared. But most of the seasonal and secular celebrations continued, especially the dancing and the singing. Like the dance, the folk song was ancient, possibly of religious origin, but generally speaking it may be regarded as 'a song born of and used by the people as an expression of their emotions and for lyrical narrative'.* A few of the ballads spring from the time when minstrels entertained the company at table with chants and tales of heroism and adventure. The majority of folk songs are post-medieval with subjects ranging over the whole of human life: songs about love, war, the sea, about the labours and sorrows of country life

* Quoted from *English Folk Song and Dance* by Frank Kidson and Mary Neal (C.U.P.).

(or – like the harvest home – about its joys), songs about sport, poaching, drinking, and death. Carols, too, were popular, and were sung not only at Christmas but at any time as an accompaniment to the dance. Soon after the invention of printing it became the fashion to publish folk songs. Usually they appeared as broadsheets, that is, they were printed on one side of the paper for ease of handling and display. Izaak Walton wrote in *The Compleat Angler*: 'I will now lead you to an honest ale-house where we shall find a cleanly room, lavender in the windows, and twenty ballads stuck about the wall.' Song publishers were either small local printers or, as in later years, large London or provincial houses that specialized in the trade. This accounts for the fact that so many 'county' songs were merely local versions of songs originating in other parts of the countryside, and subsequently mass-produced. Distribution was almost entirely in the hands of peddlers who sold the broadsheets either singly or in collections known as 'garlands'. These men toured all round the villages and fairs, especially the Hiring, Mop, or Statute Fairs, so called after the Statutes of Labourers issued in the fourteenth century, which sought to fix wages by regulation. These were held once or twice yearly, at Michaelmas and Whitsun, and were attended by farmers and by farm servants – the cowman with a wisp of straw, the shepherd with his crook – seeking fresh employment. Sometimes a Runaway Mop was held a week or two later for the benefit of those who had made a bad bargain. Such were the arrangements previous to the advertisement and the labour exchange, in which ceremony and conviviality played an equal part.

The customs of the countryside are so numerous and so various that any attempt at complete classification or definition would plainly be impossible. Reference has been made to those practised in honour of fertility; but even in other cases where the primitive origin is difficult to discern, there is an element that reflects in some degree man's ultimate dependence upon the functions of the earth. One example connected with property is the Hungerford Hocktide Festival.* This is still held about ten days after Easter, and commemorates the granting by John of Gaunt of certain fishing rights in the River Kennet, and of a large piece of waste land for use as a cattle-common. Proceedings are simpler than in the past, but the chief figures include the Constable, the Port Reeve, the Bailiff, the Bellman who sounds John of Gaunt's horn, and the two Tuttimen who, armed with gaily decorated poles, indulge in a good deal of horseplay round the town. A Banquet is held and two courts are summoned to elect the officials, decide the lettings, and generally administer the property. Another property custom is that of beating the parish bounds. This is an inheritance of the days when maps were neither plentiful nor accurate, and when it was incumbent on the vestry to prevent encroachment upon parish territory. The usual practice was an annual perambulation led by the parson and the churchwardens, and attended by a large following from the village. A point was always made of taking as many boys as possible in order that they, the future generation, might become acquainted with the appropriate landmarks, hedges, and boundary stones which defined the limits of the parish area. Sometimes the boys were beaten or bumped en route, the better to fix these matters in their minds. In some places the custom was combined with the mid-May festival of Rogation, when the fields and crops were formally blessed, and this is the form in which it still survives today.

---

*I am indebted to Major H. Fairfax Harvey, Constable of Hungerford, for a full account of the proceedings, to which I can make only a brief reference here.

Apart from custom there is another side of village social life in which tradition has always exercised a strong influence. This is sport, which has done much both to shape the character of the countryman and to reflect the nature of the society of which he is a member. Among the field sports, hunting — whether of wolf, boar, deer, or fox — always remained the prerogative of the gentry, although within certain limits everyone who cared to was allowed to play a minor part. On the other hand most villagers indulged, legally or otherwise, in trapping, ferreting, and fishing, not only as an amusement, but also as a means of staving off starvation. Thus it was that the game laws, which inflicted savage penalties on transgressors for close on a thousand years, never succeeded in eradicating what was both a passion and a necessity. Ultimately poaching was controlled by economic factors — by Enclosure and the active reclamation of waste land, and by the general improvement in standards of living; at the same time field sports gradually lost the exclusively class character they once possessed. As to athletics and games of skill, these have always flourished in all strata of rural society. Here, too, regional monopolies existed — wrestling in Cumberland and Cornwall, cudgel play and backswording in Somerset and the south Midlands, while in many parts there were well-established prototypes of the team games played today. Thus cricket may have evolved out of stoolball, already popular in the seventeenth century in the south and south-east, and football is thought to have sprung from the wild inter-village mêlées that took place every year on Shrove Tuesday. Others such as golf, hockey, and tennis have even earlier ancestries. As to military pastimes the countryman has never been backward in these. Before the introduction of firearms every man was an archer and practised assiduously at the village butts under the strict surveillance of the constable. Subsequently rifle shooting became popular, and many parishes still have their own ranges with thriving clubs to patronize them. Nowadays the old village sports have quite disappeared – tipcat, trap-ball, the Yorkshire game of knurr and spell, and all the traditional contests such as Thomas Hughes described in his account of the last 'Scouring' of the Uffington White Horse in 1857. Football in winter, cricket in summer, these are now the main organized recreations of the country-side, as they are of the town.

Again, no account of the social background of the village would be complete without some reference to the inn. Much has been written upon this subject and much romance conjured up where none exists. Nevertheless the plain fact is that the inn is probably the oldest institution in the village, older even than the church, and dates back to the Roman period when places of rest and refreshment were established along the newly built roads. However, the history of the inn, in its precise sense as a house of shelter for travellers, lies outside the scope of this chapter. Except in villages situated on the highways the average country inn or 'pub' was little more than an ale-house dispensing home-brewed beer to local company; and until the middle of the sixteenth century requiring no licence to do so. Its sign may have been the original of all inn-signs, the 'Bush', a symbolic bunch of ivy and vine leaves hung on an ale-stick outside the door. Like the barber's pole, it was a trade-mark that the illiterate could understand. On the other hand it may have acquired any one of a multitude of signs as a result perhaps of its association with the estate of a noble family (Craven Arms), or with a craft (Jolly Miller); or one merely adopted in honour of a hero (Duke of Welling-ton) or of the local sport (Angler's Rest). In summer the customers sat on forms outside. In winter they warmed themselves in front of the open kitchen fire, their backs shielded from the draught by the high settles. Above their heads were suspended the hams and flitches from the pig the landlord killed last month, and a row of pewter mugs from which all good ale was drunk. However, not only did the inn supply the mental and material comforts of warmth, drink, and pleasant company, but it was also the place where, for instance, the labourer aired his grievances and first felt his way towards emancipation. It was the place where humble funds were accumulated out of pennies and half-pennies to pay for the sickness or burial of a contributor, or for clothing and coal. It was the countryman's own club, a place where, free from interference and patronage, he could call his soul his own.

The case was somewhat different where other village institutions were concerned, especially those originating in the Victorian era, when enlightened patronage was expected of the gentry. Indeed patronage was the price of position, part of the established order which everyone took for granted. An outstanding example was the Flower Show and Fête, an annual event organized by a committee under the chairmanship of the squire or the parson or even the doctor. Such was the case at the village of St Mary Bourne in Hampshire, as described by Kathleen E. Innes in her book *Life in a Hampshire Village**:

About fifty years ago the village Flower Show was the great summer event. A marquee was hired to protect exhibits from sun, wind and weather and beside it in the field there arrived the day before the show, a fair, with all the traditional equipment of roundabouts, swings, coconut shies and wonderful sideshows. Admission to the field was free, and excited children swarmed into it. Pennies saved up for months soon vanished in rides on the shiny-painted horses of the roundabout, which went round and

*Privately printed.

round to the droning music, working up to what to the riders seemed a terrifying speed and then slowing down to the stopping point, and depositing giddy children on the grass again, to fill up with another load. Amid shrieks and laughter, boat-shaped swings were worked up to a height far above the horizontal, till it seemed as if the occupants must fall out, but they never did. When the time paid for – strictly measured by the groundsman – was at an end, a stout board beneath each swing was raised to catch the flat bottom and, grating along it, acted as a brake which in two or three passages brought the swing to a standstill and ended the adventure.

Judging took place in the morning, and the judges, who came from outside, did not see the names of competitors till the decisions were taken. Then the cards with names were turned face upwards, ready for the rush of excited entrants as soon as the tent was open in the afternoon. Gardeners had separate classes to prevent them, through any unfair advantage, carrying away all the prizes, but many a non-gardener's exhibit would have gained the award even in the gardeners' class.

There was always a class for cakes, and a dish of boiled potatoes 'to give the women a chance', but on more than one occasion the prize for the best cake was borne away by a boy who had made up his mind to be a chef. He is still in the village. The scene inside the tent was gay and colourful. Vases of mixed flowers, the best table decorations, bowls of roses, sprays of sweet peas, were placed to meet the eye on entering. Classes of vegetables were in their allotted places on long tables round the edge – marvellous marrows, spotless and shapely potatoes, peas and beans with pods full from top to toe; cabbages solid as cannon balls, cauliflowers round and comely, carrots long and straight. All these were set out as an inspiration and a challenge. Their owners hovered with pride near at hand to hear the freely-expressed envy and admiration.

When the exhibits were removed and the tent left empty, the fair went gaily on till the summer nightfall, the monotonous music of the roundabouts inviting all and sundry to stay and make an evening of it, for it would be gone on the morrow. It was late before even the tired and happy children went to bed.

The Chairman of the Flower Show committee was Dr Joseph Stevens, a remarkable man, who wrote *The Parochial History of St Mary Bourne*,* a model village history, and who made several social experiments of great interest and value. He organized a library in an old school building, and in 1860 founded a village museum. He was also responsible for a 'Labouring Men's Association', which held 'evening meetings for the benefit and instruction of labouring people by means of lectures, reading, etc.'. In another village in the neighbouring county, the parson financed the cricket club, lent it his glebe field on Saturday afternoons, and entertained the players to tea. In many places a public hall was built by the squire, for use as a general meeting place, for dances, receptions, lectures, for concerts by the Village Band, and for all sorts of entertainment. Such were the beginnings of modern recreation in the village. Nowadays it may be difficult at first glance to notice any changes in these matters, whereas in fact there has been a revolution. With the decline of the old rural hierarchy the element of patronage has largely disappeared. The Village Hall and the Playing Field are both democratic institutions and their maintenance is in the hands of a representative committee. The clubs and societies — too numerous to list here — exist for every purpose, for both sexes, for old and young. Few are privately subsidized as in the past, but depend on membership subscriptions supplemented by takings from organized entertainments. Some exert an influence on national affairs, the British Legion for instance, or the Women's Institutes, which have a membership of over 300,000. All this is part of the democratic development of the village, at which some may express regret. But the fact remains that if the village is to survive as a living community and not as a collection of dead stones,

*Whiting & Co.

such changes are inevitable. The countryman, too, is changing, although slowly. For instance, he still provides a large proportion of his own amusements which, in so far as they are home made, do not seriously compete with the attractions of the town, for he manages to enjoy them both. At bottom, it is this quality of self-support that distinguishes all the social life of the village, as well as the villager himself – the human element.

PART THREE

To-day and To-morrow — An Essay

INTRODUCTION

IN Parts One and Two of this book I have endeavoured to do two things: to summarize the history of country life in England from the prehistoric beginnings until the outbreak of the Second World War; and to isolate and interpret the constituent elements of the village. It is now my intention to review the main events affecting the countryside of the period 1939–50, and to comment upon the changes that have taken place. In addition I propose to offer some tentative opinions regarding the trends of rural life and work, and to consider the future of the village as an independent community.

1939–50

It is now recognized that the declaration of war against Germany in September 1939 marked the end of that long period of economic and social neglect which had first fallen upon the English countryside in the late 1870s and, except for a short interlude at the end of the First World War, had continued virtually unbroken. At the time the restoration of agriculture was regarded only as a strategic necessity, to save valuable shipping space and generally to mitigate the effects of the air and sea blockade. Indeed, as many of the older farmers knew only too well, the economy of war had little bearing upon the economy of peace, and although the Government was making some fine promises, such promises had been made before, and they had been broken. In short, once victory had been won, what guarantee was there that the debacle of 1921 would not be repeated? However, these dark considerations did not deter the farming community at large from setting about the vast programme of expansion so urgently required in the face of emergency. At the same time the difficulties to be contended with were greater than ever. Owing to the long agricultural depression much land was out of heart, and some of it had altogether reverted to waste. Farm buildings and other fixed capital equipment were in a poor state, some of it untouched since the halcyon days of the 1860s. The number of farmworkers had declined to little over half a million, or some 100,000 less than in 1921. There was an acute lack of machinery, fertilizers, and feeding stuffs. Worst of all, owing to building and industrial activity between the two wars, over a million acres of fair cultivable land had been lost to agriculture, and even more would have to be handed over, temporarily at any rate, for aerodromes and training grounds.

In spite of this, agricultural production was greatly increased, basically by means of subsidies and price controls which restored the financial incentive to farming, but also by other means. Farmwork was reserved and could not, without special permission, be exchanged for another occupation. This had the effect first of stabilizing and later of raising the regular labour force, which was soon reinforced by the Women's Land Army and by prisoners of war. Farmers were actively assisted and supervised by newly instituted County War Agricultural Executive Committees, through which the Government kept a firm hand on farming policy and progress.* These Committees also undertook large reclamation projects and contract work, established machinery pools for the hiring of implements,

* See *A Farmer in Whitehall*, by Anthony Hurd (Country Life).

and managed a number of farms where the occupiers had been dispossessed for bad husbandry. Lastly, a tremendous effort was sustained by everyone connected with the land. It is difficult even with the aid of official statistics to take stock of the progress that was made. Perhaps the most striking conclusion is the fact that by 1945 the nation was receiving two-thirds of its total food requirements from home sources, whereas the corresponding figure in 1939 had been little more than one-third. Undoubtedly some of this extra production was uneconomic and would never have been countenanced in peacetime — extensive corn-growing, for instance, on steep slopes and at high altitudes, and the fact that intensive cropping of what had formerly been indifferent grassland soon exhausted the potentialities of the ground. Yet, with all this taken into account, wartime farming proved one thing — that the land was an immense and neglected source of wealth, which in the altered circumstances of the post-war world would have to make a far greater contribution to the nation's trade than it had done in the immediate past.

There is no need in 1951 to underline this statement, but it is worth considering some of the factors responsible for the change. What, in short, has made agriculture necessary to our peacetime economy, other than its value as an insurance against the demands of possible future wars? In my opinion, the answer must be sought outside this country altogether, in the changing structure of international trade, and in the changing role that Britain has to play in it. For example, the surpluses of foreign food which used to be so freely and cheaply imported either no longer exist or they are less easily available. Although it is true that surpluses are again accumulating in some countries, the world at large is short of food. This is due both to maldistribution and, in some cases, to under-production; both are problems likely to be perpetuated by political differences and by growing populations. In consequence, the price of food remains high, which reduces the ability of Britain to import on a large scale, and which makes a far greater proportion of home-grown food an economic proposition. Again, partly owing to the War and partly for other reasons, many of the food-producing countries have begun programmes of industrialization. This means that they will eventually be unable to absorb such a large proportion of British manufactures. Thus we are already beginning to reap the harvest of Victorian industrial expansion; and although the final reckoning may be postponed by rising standards of living, which expand the old markets and create the new (especially in Asia, Africa, and the countries of the Commonwealth), the fact remains that Britain can never again be termed the 'workshop of the world'. We cannot, in other words, without losing our identity as a sovereign commercial power, indefinitely maintain the highly industrialized and urbanized economy to which we have become accustomed. This state of affairs was already in existence before the War, but in a less acute form. In those days it was possible to afford an adverse trade balance, since the deficiency was largely neutralized by the interest on overseas investments accumulated in the past. As a result of the War, however, these investments have been virtually exhausted, and the 'trade gap' has hitherto been made good only by American help and by re-armament. It is certain, therefore, that sooner or later means will have to be found of relieving the present extreme dependence upon exports. In any event, whatever the short- or long-term solution of the problem, the claims of a fully developed home agriculture (and this will be discussed further) are on economic grounds alone too strong to be set aside.

These, then, are some of the considerations which contributed to the passing in 1947 and 1948 respectively of the Agriculture Act and the Agricultural Holdings Act: legislation that bids fair to secure the stability and the prospects that are vital to a solvent agriculture and a contented countryside. In detail this includes a system of guaranteed prices fixed yearly in advance, financial assistance in the form of subsidies and grants, particularly for capital projects such as land drainage, piped water, and the reclamation of waste land, the continuance of County Agricultural Executive Committees, the setting up of a National Agricultural Advisory Service, the provision of small-holdings on a wider scale and on more generous terms to enable the enterprising farmworker to climb the ladder to independence, and increased security of tenure for the tenant farmer. Although it is still too early to pass judgement on all these provisions, there is no doubt that they have instilled great confidence in the future. Furthermore the revival of agriculture has had a widespread influence upon the whole of rural and village life. It has given new opportunities to all those crafts and industries which serve farming, in particular to the blacksmith and agricultural engineer, the carpenter-wheelwright, the thatcher, the small builder and the sawmill. It has raised the entire buying power of the countryside, where the effects may be seen, for instance, in the increased comforts and possessions of families, in the better clothing of the children, and in the larger custom bestowed upon tradesmen serving the village.

The problems of agriculture, however, cannot be confined to matters of administration and production, for there is another question which affects the very existence of farming, and ultimately that of every employment in the country. This is the question of land use. Future historians will surely look back with astonishment at the irresponsible fashion in which land was developed during the nineteenth and early twentieth centuries. In an intensely populated and industrialized country like ours the demand for land has naturally been heavy, and yet until the Second World War no *serious* attempt was ever made to exercise any control over its disposal. By then tremendous damage had been done to the limited stock of fertile soil, to the condition of agriculture, and to the general beauty of the countryside. A small part of the blame may certainly be apportioned to the farmers, who found it difficult in bad times to resist tempting offers from building speculators and others; but the major part belongs to townsmen in general, who continue to regard land as an ordinary piece of merchandise from which profits must be extracted. The fact is, of course, that land is a heritage beyond price, and that to trade it away without regard to its value to the community is an atrocious crime. For a number of years a handful of influential men and women doggedly proclaimed this point of view, and the existence of voluntary bodies such as the National Trust and the Council for the Preservation of Rural England is evidence of their efforts. But the results achieved were infinitesimal in relation to the problem of land planning as a whole. The long tradition of *laissez-faire* in all matters pertaining to commerce was too strong to break down in a short time, and so the by-passes continued to be built up and bungalows scattered at random over a fair landscape. Once again what was considered impossible in peace was achieved in war, and the conception of planning acknowledged, which had so long been urged by such men as Sir Patrick Abercrombie, the late Mr John Dower, Dr Thomas Sharp, Mr Clough Williams-Ellis, and Professor Dudley Stamp, who on his own initiative had organized a national land utilization survey in the 1930s. In 1941 two Committees were appointed by the Minister of Works to make a preliminary investigation. The first, under the Chairmanship of the Hon. Mr Justice Uthwatt, was 'to make an objective analysis of the subject of the payment of compensation and recovery of betterment in respect of public control of the use of land'. The second, under the Chairmanship of the Rt Hon. Lord Justice Scott, was 'to consider the conditions which should govern building and other constructional development in country areas consistently with the maintenance of agriculture, and in particular the factors affecting the location of industry, having regard to economic operation, part-time and seasonal employment, the well-being of rural communities and the preservation of rural amenities'. The reports were published in the following year, and although not adopted wholesale, they were in the main accepted by Parliament, which created a new Ministry with sole responsibility for planning. In 1947 the Town and Country Planning Act was passed, which formally placed the control of land use in the hands of the public. In fact planning powers were delegated for the most part to County and County Borough Councils, which were then placed under obligation to make definite proposals for their areas. The Act also stated the terms of the compensation payable to owners who stood to lose the development value of their properties, for this was henceforth to accrue to the State as a 'development charge'. At the time of writing it is difficult to gauge the success of the Act. It was violently opposed in Parliament, and it undoubtedly led to many rigid and petty restrictions, many of which have now been abolished. On the other hand this was to be expected from such a revolutionary and complex piece of legislation and an amending Act may have to be considered. Nevertheless it has succeeded in establishing a principle essential to the survival of agriculture and of the right use of the countryside at large. Moreover, if it is in the details of administration that the greatest difficulties lie, then as much depends upon the wisdom of the administrators as upon the wording of the regulations. Plainly it is impossible to fix in advance such matters as the priorities that have to be allotted to the legitimate claims of agriculture, forestry, mining, roads, industry, towns, villages, or military training, in any one area. Controversy is inevitable, but that does not reflect adversely upon the necessity for planning; on the contrary it is an essential method of solving problems.

Finally no account of the period would be complete without a reference to the principal changes in the social life of the countryside. Materially, despite shortages and restrictions, considerable progress has been made. As soon as the War was over, electricity, gas, water, and the telephone and public transport services were all extended on a large scale, and village housing schemes were put in hand by Rural District Councils. A notable feature of the new 'Council' houses was the improved standard of exterior and interior design, especially the provision made to meet the practical needs of the farmworker. As to social legislation – health insurance, public assistance, family allowances, etc. – these benefits have been enjoyed as much in the country as in the town. Perhaps the two Acts of Parliament that affected the countryside most were the Education Act, 1944, which has already been discussed in Part Two, Chapter 4, and the National Parks and Access to the Countryside Act, 1949. This is so recently on the Statute Book that little has so far been accomplished beyond setting up the administrative machinery, designating some of the National Park areas, and instituting a survey of all the rights of way. These are vital matters touching the most delicate relationships of townsman and countryman. In one sense the townsman gains most, for he now has the full authority of

Parliament to enjoy the amenities of the countryside. For that reason the countryman is apprehensive. He anticipates hooliganism, especially if he lives in the neighbourhood of a town. This is a real danger, although it possibly may be less in the National Parks, many of which are wild moorlands, where comparatively little damage can be done. In the cultivated countryside it is quite another matter. Apart from malicious damage, much trouble can be caused by carelessness and ignorance, leaving gates open or straying off the paths on to arable ground. There is also another aspect to the question. With the advent of cars and bicycles country people walk far less than in the past, and in many parishes perhaps only a quarter of the public paths are in use, the rest are obsolete and overgrown. Ramblers, on the other hand, and all those townspeople who enjoy walking in the countryside, are on the increase, and they are rightly anxious that the paths be kept open. It is to be hoped then that a compromise may be reached, and that every parish will, besides retaining paths of purely local use, preserve one or two 'through paths' to enable strangers to reach the neighbouring parishes on foot. As for the rest, if they are inconvenient or no longer used, then they should be altered or abolished, for rights of way are not sacrosanct, but should always serve a useful purpose. Yet, with all the objections, the survey is much to be welcomed. It is the necessary preliminary to the drawing up of an official record which will automatically resolve all future doubts as to which are the public rights of way, and this is long overdue.

THE FUTURE

THE LAND

The land (in the form of agriculture, forestry, and associated work) must clearly remain the chief single source of employment in the countryside, although, except perhaps in the most remote areas, it can never be the only one. Furthermore, if agriculture (as representative of all landwork) is to maintain prosperity without undue dependence upon special subsidies (e.g. lime, calf-rearing, etc., which assist the farmer, not the consumer), it will have to intensify production. Paradoxically enough this cannot be done by increasing the number of agriculturists without affecting the standard of living, for in this country economic efficiency must always depend upon as high an output as possible per acre and per man. In my view then the present total of approximately one million farmers and farmworkers in England and Wales is unlikely to rise, while the area of fair agricultural land may, owing to the legitimate demands of towns and industry, contract to as little as 20 million acres. That will not be altogether a calamity if it is accompanied by intelligent mechanization and management, by the encouragement of invention and research, by the simplification of marketing, and by certain fundamental reforms in the structure of farms. At present the drawing of property boundaries is left to the whims of the estate market, with the result that few farms can be described as good workable units. In the same way the majority of fields were laid out in the days of hand and horse power, and are unsuited to modern implements. Again another embarrassment is to be found in the buildings, often too solidly constructed and difficult to adapt. Nowadays standard units are required, with many uses, and perhaps not too permanent. As to the type of farming to be practised, that is really a matter outside the scope of this book; nevertheless there are certain considerations that cannot be ignored. Ours is a small island with a heavy urban economy, having a limited amount of agricultural land. This dictates a policy of crop and stock husbandry that will give most value from the small area available, and which is suitable in terms of climate and soil. In the long run this points to the predominance of grass, dairy cattle, pigs, poultry, and the production of market garden crops, although this certainly does not preclude other activities where local conditions permit. Such a policy would allow for profits and wages comparable with those in the town, and this in turn would enable the countryside to afford many of the material benefits that now have to be provided at the expense of the taxpayer. Much has been written about the rural 'way of life', perhaps too much. At the same time it is true that there are certain advantages, some of them intangible, to be gained from living and working in the country — sound health, a keen appreciation of Nature, and an intimate sense of community, to name but a few — and these may always have to redress a slight disparity in the standard of living between country and town. Besides this, the land must continue to find room for a small proportion of smallholdings, which have a social rather than an economic value, but it would be wrong to regard this as an important element in the future. Farming must, like any other industry, be economically sound. It must not and cannot be preserved for the sake, say, of tradition or aesthetics. The country is not a museum.

CRAFTS, INDUSTRY, AND TRADE

In the past agriculture was scarcely more able than it is now, having regard to the larger population, to provide employment for the whole of the countryside. Men and women not working on the land earned their living at a number of occupations, of which a large part can be termed 'industrial' in the widest sense. A leading element in this category was the handicrafts and small enterprises concerned with production of tools, equipment, clothing, and many other goods which now issue from large-scale industry. To a much reduced extent, however, this situation still holds good, and I foresee a future for most craftsmen serving the needs of agriculture, particularly the blacksmith and agricultural engineer. Also, in certain parts of the country where there are good sources of raw material (e.g. osiers for basket-making in the Somerset fens), or where there is a traditional market (e.g. rope and netting in fishing villages), it is likely that the trade will continue. Again it is possible that the demand will grow for the hand-made as opposed to the factory-made article, especially where quality and not price is the first consideration. The Rural Industries Bureau, which is a Government-sponsored organization, is much alive to the potentialities of this situation, and is doing everything to exploit it. Likewise the Women's Institutes encourage cottage industry among village women, for both its practical and its cultural value. Even so handicrafts are not likely to recover the importance they once had in providing 'industrial' employment in the village.

In similar case are those small-scale *rural* industries (i.e. those making use of the raw materials of the countryside) which may be concerned with one or more of the following:

(a) The extraction of raw material (timber from a forest, slate or stone from a quarry, clay from a pit, etc.).

(b) The manufacture of goods from the raw material (all wood products, bricks, tiles, lime, etc.).

(c) The processing or packing of food (canning, a creamery, etc.).

It is possible that in some areas and in some villages the balance of labour may be absorbed by work of this nature. But as a general rule it is not so, a fact that has contributed as much as the decline of agriculture to the drift from the countryside in the past. This is a problem which must be solved if the village is to survive in any form as a solvent economic unit.

One solution is to introduce light industry. To many people this idea is repugnant, generally because such factories as have been built in villages up to now are ugly and tend to overawe the neighbourhood. Defects like these have arisen because the factories have arrived by chance and not by design. There are, however, several alternatives if planning is employed. For instance, a single factory can be limited in size to 50 or 60 hands, and several such factories planted in an area, one in each main village. A scheme of this kind avoids denuding other occupations, it prevents too great a dependence upon one industry (thus mitigating the effects of a slump), it provides diversity of employment and opens up new opportunities for country children leaving school, it may provide part-time employment which is sometimes needed in a village, it certainly provides a reserve of labour to help farmers with the hay and corn harvest in the evenings and at weekends, and it keeps the development of the village within bounds. Finally there is no reason why a rural factory should not be well sited and designed, and add to rather than detract from the harmony of the scene.

A second solution is to concentrate all light industry in small country towns and staff it with workers who come in every day from surrounding villages. This is the normal practice today, and applies not only to light industry but to all kinds of non-agricultural employment. Often it is the only practicable solution, but dangers arise where labour has to be drawn from long distances. In that case a countryman who spends several hours a day travelling to and from his work tends to lose contact with his own village, and in the end he removes for the sake of convenience to the town where his work is situated.

Finally there is yet one more field in which rural employment may be found. This is the retail trade of the countryside or 'service' industry, as it is called in planning parlance. It includes shops, public services, and all those undertakings which cater for the *everyday* needs of country people. As an example, I will quote the case of an actual South Midland village, with an approximate population of 1200, which supports the following businesses:

2 butchers, 2 bakers, 1 newsagent-stationer, 1 draper, 4 grocers, 2 confectioner-tobacconists (one is a barber as well), 1 tailor, 1 coal merchant, 1 fruit and fishmonger, 1 cycle and radio shop, 1 garage, 2 builders, 1 haulier, 1 post office, 6 inns. In addition there are several visiting craftsmen, a timber yard, and a flour mill employing 30 hands, mostly girls.

Most of the shops are family concerns, while none employs more than six people altogether. Duplication of bakers, grocers, and butchers is desirable in a village where acquaintance is close, and minor altercations easily arise; to remain on friendly terms is often difficult if there is no freedom of choice. Theoretically there is still room for new businesses – a chemist, a shoe-repairer, an ironmonger, possibly a laundry. In addition some of the existing concerns might well extend their scope. Here, then, is a concrete case where a village has succeeded in retaining the bulk of its retail trade, so often monopolized by the nearest town. It is a lesson to be learnt in many other places which suffer from a lack of alternative employment to agriculture. However, not every village can provide sufficient custom to justify development of this kind. It is primarily a question of population, and this will be discussed further.

VILLAGE LIFE

In the country as in the town, remunerative work is the foundation upon which the rest of life is built. Without it there can be no facilities for and no expression of civilized life of any kind — no houses, no comforts, no leisure, and no future. This is, of course, a truism, but after seventy years of rural neglect it needs constant emphasis in order that the *causes* of neglect shall never again be misunderstood, and the past repeated in the future. Once the economic foundation has been laid, then it is possible to build socially. Furthermore, without a proper social order, no workman (of any kind or station) can lead a satisfactory existence or remain at his work. What, then, is the social order of the countryside? In my view it is an expression synonymous with village life, for although many areas are sparsely populated the bulk of the rural population live in villages, and it is there that the 'social order' exists. This, therefore, is the real meaning and purpose of the village. It is the community that, in large measure, provides country people with not only the facilities and amenities of life but also the corporate sense that arises from proximity and association. The decline of the village is one of the tragedies of English history, no less tragic because it is largely unrecognized. Now that this decline is being arrested, and there are prospects of revival, it is essential to comprehend the new situation and to revive the village in a manner that is consistent with modern conditions and trends. For this reason I propose to review those aspects of village life which have a direct bearing upon the future.

In the physical development of the village a strong effort must be made to concentrate and integrate the component elements. The defects of ribbon and sporadic building are now generally appreciated, but apart from economy in the use of land, the convenience and the accessibility which result from a reasonable density of building contribute directly to the corporate strength of the community. Again the shape of the village has a direct bearing upon its vitality. While the *street* form tends to deteriorate into a ribbon, the *square* has many advantages. Chiefly it lends itself to the creation of a strong focus, such as a green or open space. Traditionally this has always proved a great asset to village life, and one which, in the case of a Playing Field, will satisfy a great recreational need in the future. Then there are several buildings which, if topography allows, can also be sited in the centre. One such building is obviously the Village Hall, which can serve a number of useful purposes. The possibilities include medical consulting rooms, Parish Council offices, or a local museum, all additional to the accepted range of accommodation — the assembly hall and stage, committee rooms, the canteen, and so forth, which cater for all the normal communal activities of the village. Similar advantages accrue from accessibility in the case of other village buildings and institutions — the church or chapel, the inn, the school, the post office, and the shops. It is one reason why 'tied' cottages on farms should be kept at a minimum and confined to key workers, such as foremen and stockmen, who by virtue of their higher pay can afford the inconveniences occasioned by distance from the village and its amenities. On the other hand deliberate class segregation should be avoided — 'Council' houses in one part, private villas and bungalows in another; it does nothing to improve class relations, it has no historical justification, and it is usually hideous. No less distressing is the type of architecture that either apes the past or misconstrues the present; too often there is no attempt at design at all. A village must achieve harmony, not necessarily by uniformity but by the integration of genuine contemporary styles.

I believe, then, that by physical means much can be done to assist the regeneration of village life, but regeneration cannot depend upon physical means alone. Other steps must be taken to revitalize the principal institutions, and to recreate a sense of responsibility, formerly the prerogative of the upper ranks of the social hierarchy.

Take the Church as an example. Often a country parish of less than a thousand inhabitants does not provide a resident parson with enough work. That is, frequently, the reason why so many country parsons are regarded with indifference and contempt. In the old days the priest farmed his own glebe, and although a cow might calve during the service and interfere with his meditations, at least time did not hang heavy on his hands. Nowadays the Church is not in a position to buy back its own land, and in any event that is not the right solution. It would be far better to re-organize the parish system, and either allot a man several parishes in plurality (and this is a practice already being adopted, but under compulsion), or serve a large area from a central headquarters staffed by itinerant clergymen. In either case the parson would be a less frequent figure in the village, but he would lose little of his scope for leadership and example.

Take the Parish Council. In Part Two, Chapter 3, an account has been given of its principal powers. These are not large, but in general they have not been exercised to their fullest extent, and parish councillors have insufficient knowledge of the actions that are open to them. No doubt they are discouraged by the drift towards the centralization of authority, which in the countryside is being vested more and more in the hands of the County Council. Nevertheless there is still plenty of room for reform in parish administration. For example the Parish Council could become the agent of the County Council and perform several duties for which the latter has insufficient time and staff. The repair of by-roads is one possibility, and this might well be carried out under local arrangements far more expeditiously than at present. Already under the provisions of the National Parks and Access to the Countryside Act the Parish Council is acting in this capacity as regards rights of way, for although the County Council is ultimately responsible for all highways it cannot possibly oversee all matters of local detail. This would, of course, necessitate increased spending powers on the part of the Parish Council, which should be able to raise up to a 1s. 6d. rate, reinforced by grants where required. But there are other cheaper and less burdensome ways in which the Council can expand its activities. It can become the repository of local history. The Clerk could keep a diary of events, both those which occur within the village and the manner in which outside affairs, wars or Jubilees, for example, affect village life. This might develop into the publication of an occasional magazine, well printed and attractively presented, containing news about the whole village. It would engender much enthusiasm, and it might possibly sow the seeds of a local culture. It is in these days of disruptive social change that a truly democratic institution such as the Parish Council must advance. It is there that some of the new leaders will have to be found, to take up the responsibilities at present shouldered by a faithful but declining minority.

These are but two examples of the manner in which village institutions might be reinvigorated.

How far will the village succeed in regaining the vitality it once possessed? Even if there is economic and social progress along the lines I have suggested, will it be sufficient? No definite answer is possible. The days of literal self-sufficiency are plainly over, but that does not prevent the development of the village within a limited framework of independence. All modern life is the same. We draw what we can from the material benefits and intellectual stimuli that derive from our national existence, but we are still individuals. So it is with the village, where it is *mental* independence that matters, for only by the rationalization of *physical* resources will survival be possible at all. For instance, villages of less than 500 inhabitants are not usually able to afford the upkeep of all the services, amenities, and institutions that give a place a strength and a character of its own. There is not enough work, not enough custom for village trade, not enough patronage of village societies, not enough children for the primary schools, not enough life. This is a solid fact that cannot be abolished by sentiment or by appeals to the ancient heritage of village history. Only by a sensible alliance of neighbouring settlements in these matters can the tiniest hamlet retain a vestige of personality. Size is not sacrosanct, and self-sufficiency is impossible. Our aim must be an integrated rural community.

A SELECTIVE BIBLIOGRAPHY

The books listed here are my personal choice only. They do not cover the whole subject; that would be impossible within a reasonable compass, and a comprehensive Bibliography would be so long as to defeat the purpose of the book. This, therefore, is intended as a basic guide, particularly to those readers who may be interested in pursuing a little further some single aspect of village life. The titles marked with an asterisk are regarded as introductory.

THE HISTORY OF FARMING

English Farming, Past and Present by Lord Ernle. Longmans.

A History of English Farming by C. S. Orwin. Nelson.*

A History of Agriculture by T. Bedford Franklin. Bell.*

Rural England by H. Rider Haggard. Longmans.

The Evolution of the English Farm by M. E. Seebohm.

Farm History by Grant Uden. Methuen.*

Plough and Pasture by E. C. Curwen. Cobbett Press.

The Open Fields by C. S. and C. S. Orwin. O.U.P.

English Field Systems by H. L. Gray. Harvard Historical Studies.

Thomas Tusser by Dorothy Hartley. Country Life.

The Old English Farming Books (Fitzherbert to Tull 1523–1730) by G. E. Fussell. Crosby Lockwood.

More Old English Farming Books (Tull to Board of Agriculture 1731–1793) by G. E. Fussell. Crosby Lockwood.

English Husbandry by Robert Trow-Smith. Faber.

THE SOCIAL AND ECONOMIC HISTORY OF THE COUNTRYSIDE

English Social History by G. M. Trevelyan. Longmans.

The English Village Community by F. Seebohm. O.U.P.

Prehistoric Britain by Jacquetta and Christopher Hawkes. Chatto and Windus, Penguin Books.

Roman Britain and the English Settlements by R. G. Collingwood and J. N. L. Myres. O.U.P.

Anglo-Saxon England by F. M. Stenton. O.U.P.

A History of Everyday Things in England (4 vols.) by Marjorie and C. H. B. Quennell. Batsford.

Foundations of Agricultural Economics by J. A. Venn. C.U.P.

An Introduction to the Economic History of England by E. Lipson. A. & C. Black.

A Short Economic History of England by Charlotte M. Waters. Clarendon Press.*

An Economic Geography of Great Britain by Wilfred Smith. Methuen.

Life and Work of the People of England (6 vols.) by Dorothy Hartley and Margaret M. Elliott. Batsford.

The Village Labourer by J. L. and Barbara Hammond. Guild Books.

The English Rural Labourer by G. E. Fussell. Batchworth.

Sharpen the Sickle by Reg. Groves. Porcupine Press.*

From Tolpuddle to T.U.C. by G. E. Fussell. Windsor Press.*

A History of the English Agricultural Labourer by W. Hasbach. Staples.

Village Life by Norman Wymer. Harrap.*

The Englishman's Food by J. C. Drummond and Anne Wilbraham. Cape.

The English Countryman: A Study of the English Tradition
by H. J. Massingham. Batsford.

A Land by Jacquetta Hawkes. Cresset Press.

A Country Parish by A. W. Boyd. Collins.

VILLAGE ADMINISTRATION AND RECORDS

The Parish Chest by W. E. Tate. C.U.P.*

The Publications of the Parish Councils Association.*

The Roscoe Lecture 1949 by the Rt Hon. Sir Leslie
Scott. Literary and Philosophical Society of Liverpool.

Parish Councillor's Guide by F. L. Edwards. Shaw and
Sons.

Dumsday's Parish Councils Handbook by Desmond Neligan.
Hadden Best.

The Care of County Muniments by G. Herbert Fowler.
County Councils Association.

RELIGION IN THE VILLAGE

A History of the English Church (8 vols.) edited by the Very
Rev. W. R. W. Stephens and the Rev. William Hunt.
Macmillan.

The English Country Parson by William Addison. Dent.

The Old-Time Parson by P. H. Ditchfield. Methuen.

The Parish Clerk by P. H. Ditchfield. Methuen.

Christianity in England by C. A. Alington. Clarendon
Press.*

The Parish Churches of England by J. C. Cox and C. B.
Ford. Batsford.

The Parish Church by P. Thornhill. Methuen.*

The Free Church Tradition in the Life of England by E. A.
Payne. S.C.M. Press.

LAND USE AND RURAL PLANNING

Town and Country Planning by Sir Patrick Abercrombie. O.U.P.

Planning and the Countryside by Jaqueline Tyrwhitt. Art and Educational Publishers.*

The Anatomy of the Village by Thomas Sharp. Penguin Books.*

English Panorama by Thomas Sharp. Architectural Press.

Town and Countryside by Thomas Sharp. O.U.P.

Town Planning by Thomas Sharp. Penguin Books.

Britain's Town and Country Pattern, prepared by Nuffield College Social Reconstruction Survey. Faber & Faber.

The Land of Britain: Its Use and Misuse by L. Dudley Stamp. Longmans.

Village and Town by S. R. Badmin. Penguin Books.*

Notes on the Siting of Houses in Country Districts. Ministry of Town and Country Planning. H.M.S.O.

VILLAGE BUILDINGS

The English Cottage by H. Batsford and C. Fry. Batsford.*

English Village Homes by Sydney R. Jones. Batsford.

Old English Household Life by Gertrude Jekyll and Sydney R. Jones. Batsford.

English Villages and Hamlets by Humphrey Pakington. Batsford.

Housing the Country Worker by M. F. Tilley. Faber & Faber.*

Country Cottages by Marshall Sisson. Methuen.*

Evolution of the English House by S. O. L. Addy. Allen & Unwin.

The Development of English Building Construction by C. F. Innocent. C.U.P.

RACE, LANGUAGE, AND PLACE-NAMES

Racial Origins of the English Character by R. N. Bradley. Allen & Unwin.

The Races of England and Wales by H. J. Fleure. Benn.*

The History of Modern Colloquial English by H. C. Wyld. Blackwell.

The English Dialect Dictionary edited by Joseph Wright. Frowde.

English Dialects from the Eighth Century to the Present Day by W. W. Skeat. C.U.P.*

English Place-Names by H. G. Stokes. Batsford.*

The Publications of the English Place-Name Society, C.U.P.

Concise Oxford Dictionary of English Place-Names by E. Ekwall. O.U.P.

A Natural History of Man in Britain by A. J. Fleure. Collins.

HANDICRAFTS AND RURAL INDUSTRIES

Rural Industries of England and Wales (4 vols.) edited by C. S. Orwin, Agricultural Economics Research Institute, Oxford. Clarendon Press.

English Country Crafts by Norman Wymer. Batsford.*

Rural Crafts of England by K. S. Woods. Harrap.*

Crafts of the Countryside by E. J. Stowe. Longmans.*

The Publications of the Rural Industries Bureau.

The Wheelwright's Shop by George Sturt. C.U.P.

The Village Carpenter by Walter Rose. C.U.P.

Country Relics by H. J. Massingham. C.U.P.

Purbeck Shop by Eric Benfield. C.U.P.

VILLAGE EDUCATION

History of Elementary Education in England and Wales by C. Birchenough. University Tutorial Press.

The Education of the Countryman by H. M. Burton. Routledge and Kegan Paul.

Our Changing Schools by Roger Armfelt. H.M.S.O.*

County Affairs by Roger Armfelt. Pilot Press.

The Dodo by Vicars Bell. Faber & Faber.

Village College by Henry Morris. O.U.P.

Pamphlets issued by the Ministry of Education since 1945.

THE SOCIAL LIFE OF THE VILLAGE

The English Inn by Thomas Burke. Longmans.

The Old Inns of England by A. E. Richardson. Batsford.*

England's Dances by Douglas Kennedy. Bell.*

English Folk-Song and Dance by Iolo A. Williams. Longmans.

English Folk-Song and Dance by Frank Kidson and Mary Neal. C.U.P.

English Sports and Pastimes by Christina Hole. Batsford.*

Old English Customs and Ceremonies by F. J. Drake-Carnell. Batsford.*

English Custom and Usage by Christina Hole. Batsford.

Hunting England by Sir William Beach Thomas. Batsford.

THE VILLAGE TODAY

The Changing Village by F. G. Thomas. Nelson.

Life in an English Village by Noel Carrington. Penguin Books.

Can Country Life Survive? by Victor Bonham-Carter. Bureau of Current Affairs Pamphlet No. 27.

The Village has a Future by Victor Bonham-Carter.
Bureau of Current Affairs Pamphlet No. 69.*
Your Village and Mine by C. H. Gardiner. Faber & Faber.*
Problems of the Countryside by C. S. Orwin. C.U.P.

Index

A New Penguin Series

THE BUILDINGS OF ENGLAND

NIKOLAUS PEVSNER

Slade Professor of Fine Art at the University of Cambridge

This series is being launched to meet a growing demand from
students and travellers for more detailed information about the
history and architecture of the buildings they visit. It will provide a complete and authoritative introduction to the churches,
monuments, and large houses, in fact to every structure of interest
in a county, from prehistoric remains to the latest building ot
note, treating them village by village and town by town, and in
the case of churches describing not only the exterior but also the
furnishings, such as pulpits, roof-bosses, plate and rood-screens.
Each volume will contain a long and general introduction to the
architectural history of the county, a map, and a large section of
illustrations. The first three volumes, at three shillings and sixpence each, are *Cornwall, Nottinghamshire*, and *Middlesex*;
North Devon, South Devon, and *London (except the City and West-
minster)* will follow early in 1952.

'Inventories these books are, and wonderfully detailed ones. But
they are much more than that. On every page one is continually
made aware – sometimes by a sentence of comment, sometimes
by as little as a single word, sometimes even by what isn't said – of
learning, intelligence and taste of work, placing, testing and
assessing. So far as architecture is concerned, this series will
relegate most other guides to the status of picture books.' –
Architects Journal.

The King Penguins

EDITED BY NIKOLAUS PEVSNER AND R. B. FISHENDEN

Described by Clive Bell as 'short, illustrated monographs, edited and written by scholars', the King Penguins were originally inspired by the Insel-Bücherei, a series published in Leipzig before the war. The sixty-odd volumes cover a wide range of subjects from *Russian Icons* to *British Beetles*, from John Piper's account in words and pictures of *Romney Marsh* to the recently published *Ackermann's Cambridge*, and in each case the colour or black-and-white illustrations have been introduced by a twenty-eight to sixty-eight page essay. Special care has been taken to use the best possible methods of reproduction and the high standard of the typography is now widely recognized. They have stiff board covers attractively designed.

Below: One of John Speed's illustrations reproduced in black and white from a colour plate in *An Atlas of Tudor England and Wales*, introduced by E. G. R. Taylor.

Two Series

THE PENGUIN HANDBOOKS

This is a series of practical manuals on gardening, farming, domestic affairs and similar matters by acknowledged experts, all written primarily for the layman who starts without any knowledge at all. They are of interest and value also to the professional, who wants some guidance on a particular question or another opinion on his subject. The volumes at present available are: *Trees and Shrubs, Soft Fruit Growing, Tree Fruit Growing* (in two volumes), *The Vegetable Grower's Handbook, The Penguin Handyman, Keeping Poultry and Rabbits on Scraps, Beekeeping, Flower Gardening, Common Sense in the Nursery, Grow Up – and Live, Successful Living*, and *The Penguin Cookery Book*. Most volumes are illustrated and the price varies between 1s 6d and 3s 6d.

THE THINGS WE SEE

'They run to sixty-four pages, and are profusely and beautifully illustrated. They are marvels of the printer's and publisher's art, and should prove extremely popular. . . . They are aids to informed understanding, they direct the eye and mind to a cultural discrimination, and all this with subtle wit, based on expert knowledge.' Thus the *British Journal of Photography* described this series, which so far includes *Indoors and Out, Houses, Furniture, Pottery and Glass, Public Transport*, and *Ships*. Each volume has been written by a specialist, and measures 8½ by 7 inches. The first volume is priced at 3s 6d and the others at 2s 6d. Another volume in the series, *Gardens*, will be published soon.

FLOWERS OF THE MEADOW

GEOFFREY GRIGSON

K 53

'Mr Grigson gives us a lively and instructive essay, . . . fittingly illustrated in the coloured plates by Robin Tanner. A charming, unpretentious book.' – *The Field.* (3s)

UNCOMMON WILD FLOWERS

JOHN HUTCHINSON

A 223

Most of the common or widely distributed wild flowers have been described and illustrated in the author's *Common Wild Flowers* (A 153) and *More Common Wild Flowers* (A 180). This volume deals with a selection of those that are less common, or common only in certain localities. With over 200 drawings by the author and thirty-two photographs. (3s)

A companion book, now available, is Florence Ranson's *British Herbs,* A 183 in the Pelican series. (1s 6d)

WILD FLOWERS OF THE CHALK

JOHN GILMOUR

K 37

'It is impossible to rate too highly the sixteen colour plates. . . . No one would fail to identify a plant thus illustrated, but apart from this, each plate is a work of art. This book, small though it is, is one which every field naturalist should possess.' – *Nature.* (2s 6d)

BIRD RECOGNITION II

JAMES FISHER

A 176

The second volume of this series, which describes the appearance, life and habits of the birds of prey and waterfowl with over eighty illustrations by 'Fish-Hawk' and many charts and maps. Volume I (A175) deals with sea birds and waders.

WATCHING BIRDS

JAMES FISHER

A 75

A description of the world of birds and of the methods and instruments people can use to get a better understanding of it. This is an enlarged and revised edition with many line drawings and diagrams. (2s)

A BOOK OF DUCKS

PHYLLIS BARCLAY-SMITH

K 58

A well-known ornithologist has here written the first monograph on Ducks within the means of the general public. It is illustrated with sixteen attractive colour plates by Peter Shepheard and many line drawings, one of which is reproduced below

MEDIEVAL PEOPLE

EILEEN POWER

A 19

An illustrated history of the Middle Ages, presented through descriptions of the daily life of various ordinary people, chosen because they represent different aspects of social life. This is the second Pelican edition. (2s)

LIFE IN SHAKESPEARE'S ENGLAND

JOHN DOVER WILSON

A 143

An anthology collected from many contemporary sources to illuminate the conditions, the appearance, the habits, pastimes and beliefs of Shakespeare's time. Below is one of the illustrations. (2s 6d)

THE WEATHER
GEORGE KIMBLE
A124

A full account of what is known about the behaviour of the weather, its science, and the methods by which the modern forecaster reaches his conclusions. A revised and enlarged edition with twenty-four illustrations is now available. (2s 6d)

GEOLOGY IN THE SERVICE OF MAN
W. G. FEARNSIDES AND O. M. B. BULMAN
A128

'An eminently readable as well as an authoritative booklet which can be commended unreservedly to those who feel hesitant about tackling the more profound text-books but who desire something more than mere generalities.' – *Engineering*. (1s 6d)

LOCAL GOVERNMENT IN ENGLAND AND WALES
W. ERIC JACKSON
A162

A simplified explanation of what the Local Government system is, its place in the national scheme, and the numerous and important public services which various types of local council perform. A new impression will be available shortly. (1s 6d)

MINERALS IN INDUSTRY
W. R. JONES
A123

A concise account of the many minerals and mineral products – such as gold, copper, zinc and salt – employed in modern commerce, describing their nature, where they are found, and their various uses and importance to man. (1s 6d)